The Social Gaia

The Social Gaia

(The little blue book for new capitalism)

Tony Jenkins

To order additional copies of this book, contact:
Xlibris Corporation
1-888-795-4274
www.Xlibris.com
Orders@Xlibris.com
57169

I dedicate this book to my grandchildren,
Thomas, Haley, Ashley and Michael.
May they grow up in a world as beautiful and exciting
as the one bequeathed to me.

Contents

Introduction

Barack Obama in his presidential election victory speech declared to the world that a "new dawn of political leadership is at hand". His victory has given new enthusiasm and hope that real change will be brought to government in Washington. At the start of the election process, all the candidates promised change, which was not surprising since most people in the U.S. recognize that the very fabric of our once vibrant democracy has been eroded and needs real change to halt the decline. Our schools have deteriorated; our international debt has exploded; our esteem in the world is at rock bottom; deaths by terrorist acts throughout the world mount daily; our healthcare system continues to fall behind almost all the other western nations; our streets are awash with cheap narcotics; the planet is being cooked by our effluent; our financial institutions have lost their integrity and threaten the very basis of capitalist society; the rich have gotten richer and the working poor are losing their homes to repossession in record numbers. We need real change to address these problems, and we live in hope that President Obama's administration will bring new vigor to find innovative solutions to them. Unfortunately, politics is an art of the possible, and some changes will be required that may be impossible within the confines of existing political and social institutions and practices. Real change to the establishment will perhaps only come by pressure from the people who are not sworn to uphold the status quo. The spirit of the people, the "yes we can" attitude so well highlighted in President elect Obama's victory speech still survives in America, but this will be sorely tried in the coming years as we begin to pay for the profligacy of our political leaders and the previous practices of the establishment.

I harbor a hope that I can offer some help in finding new innovative approaches to the pressing problems, since for most of my life, I have successfully sought innovative technical solutions to some of society's problems. I have dealt with US congressional politicians and government departments while selling innovative security products, without donating to individual politician's election funds. I have testified before Congress on anti terrorist security measures, and my own company has provided anti terrorist security to many Heads of State around the world from the Queen of England to the President of the People's Republic of China. During the last year in which I ran the company, the General and Administrative (G&A) overhead was 3% of sales. This is about five times less than most manufacturing companies, and was achieved without outsourcing any services other than treasury. A similar level of efficiency needs to be achieved in Government services if we are to remain competitive in the newly flattened world. You will find in the pages of this book many suggestions on new ways that the daunting issues of today can be addressed at the same time as government is made more efficient.

I was very fortunate in my early career in scientific instrumentation design to begin at the start of a revolutionary period in chemical analytical instrumentation. This was the period when gas chromatography and other spectrophotometric techniques were first developed by scientists and engineers who worked with great excitement and enthusiasm. I was privileged to know and work with several of the legendary researchers who made innovative contributions to the science and technology of analytical instrumentation. I learned from these original thinkers not to be constrained by prevailing technology and accepted practices. This book does not deal in any way with analytical instrumentation but uses the innovative thinking processes I learned in my own field of expertise to challenge prevailing political and social practices that do not appear to have been subjected to any really creative change since Abraham Lincoln. My aim in writing this challenge to the stagnating democracies of the western world is to encourage a dialog which may help in the reinvigoration of democratic thought and systems. The motivation for this proposal comes largely from the failures of our Western Democracies to solve many of today's issues, both spiritual and secular, at all levels, local, national, and international.

You may remark at the effrontery of a scientist/engineer who should feel competent to comment largely on U.S. political and socio economic systems. To those who do, I must point out that everyone in U.S. elected government office swears to uphold the Constitution, so we cannot look to our elected officers to initiate sweeping Constitutional changes which may be necessary to keep our Democracy fresh and buoyant. Janet Rae-Dupree, in an article in the New York Times on December 30th 2007 wrote "As our knowledge and expertise increase, our creativity and ability to innovate tend to taper off. Why? Because the walls of the proverbial box in which we think are thickening along with our experience. In other words, it becomes impossible to look beyond what you know, and think outside the box you've built around yourself." Most Americans have become comfortable, may be even complacent, within the walls of the box defined by the Constitution. These same walls have been thickened and reinforced over the last two hundred years by political and legal practices, to such an extent, that we are now prisoners behind the walls of a veritable fortress. These same walls are confining society to the social practices of the 18th and 19th centuries. Even Thomas Jefferson recognized in his own lifetime that this was becoming a problem. Forty years after he had penned the constitution, he wrote to Samuel Kercheval: "Some men look at constitutions with sanctimonious reverence and deem them like the Ark of the Covenant, too sacred to be touched. They ascribe to men of the preceding age a wisdom more than human and suppose what they did to be beyond amendment. I knew that age well; I belonged to it and labored with it. It deserved well of its country. It was very like the present but without the experience of the present; and forty years of experience in government is worth a century of book reading; and they would say themselves were they to rise from the dead."

There is a need for initiatives to break out of this confinement and seek the help of technology in devising new social and economic structures. Thomas Friedman in his excellent book "The World Is Flat" asserts that a more revealing measure of society is in the answer to the question "Does your society have more memories than dreams or more dreams than memories?" He quoted Michael Hammer, a business organization consultant who noted that "The hallmark of a truly successful organization is the willingness to abandon what made it successful and start fresh." In contrast, Theodore Dalrymple, a columnist for the London Spectator noted in the City Journal (Spring 2004) that most schools of Islam today treat the Qu'ran as a divinely inspired text that is not open to any literary criticism or creative reinterpretation. It is a sacred book to be memorized, not adapted to the demands of modern life. But without a culture that encourages, and creates a space for, such creative interpretation, critical thought and creative thinking tend to wither. John Stuart Mill put it most eloquently in his quotation "It is given to no human being to stereotype a set of truths, and walk safely by their guidance with his mind's eye closed." In the US, we are in danger of treating the Constitution as our very own

Chapter 1

The Need For Change

Not long after coming to America, I joined some colleagues in a Cranberry farming project. I was soon familiarized with the cranberry farmer's favorite saying, "if it aint broke, don't fix it". This policy seemed to work well for the cranberry farmers of Massachusetts who fixed their equipment with duck tape and baler wire when it broke. Unfortunately, most businesses fail because they fail to recognize that something is "broke" in enough time to fix it. This can be true for all organizations up to and including whole civilizations. The consistent message of Joseph A Schumpeter, the celebrated economist of the early 20th century commended the process of creative destruction. He asserted that "The very nature of fixed habits of thinking, their energy saving function, is founded upon the fact that they have become subconscious, that they yield their results automatically and are proof against criticism and even against contradiction by individual facts. But precisely because of this, they become drag-chains when they have outlived their usefulness." You may ask "why change systems that have ensured security and prosperity for decades?" The reason we need to explore fresh approaches is that many of our social systems have indeed outlived their usefulness in today's world. The world, under the flattening effect of modern transportation, the internet and global business, is changing faster today than ever before. This is causing new problems which are not being solved by society at large, and in some cases the issue is being made worse by the systems and institutions that deal with them. I would give you an example of the response to the increased threat of drugs in society. I was present at a meeting in England in 2001 where speaker after speaker stood up and reported that their anti drug initiatives with young people were not working. In fact it was shown that the DARE (drug abuse resistance education) programs not only did not succeed, they actually made the situation worse. It was determined that drug education actually encouraged the more timid students to try drugs for the first time. This is a classic case of positive feedback which I address in chapter 3, where sympathetic actions produce the opposite result to that which is intended. The situation is further exacerbated by the increased supply of both heroin and methamphetamine. Since the liberation of Afghanistan, the supply of heroin from the region has increased immensely. In March 2006, US Army LT General Karl Eikenberry, the top US commander in Afghanistan, reported that when the Taliban ran Afghanistan, its leaders enforced an effective ban on poppy growing under threat of jail. As a result, cultivation dropped to practically nothing. The State Department Annual Report on Global Narcotics published in February 2007 estimated that the Afghan opium production in 2006 surged 25% from 4,475 tonnes in 2005 to 5,644 tonnes. The resulting price on the street in both Europe and the USA has fallen to as low as $4 a sachet, and deaths due to heroin overdose are at all time highs in Europe. I doubt that anyone thought of this problem before setting out to rid Afghanistan of the Taliban and their Al Qaeda allies. The drug abuse problem is becoming the greatest threat to western democracies, exceeding that from nuclear conflict. Yet governments have been impotent to halt the increase despite incarcerating tens of thousands of people involved.

International Terrorism

Another more obvious problem which makes headlines daily is our inability to contain the threat of terrorism. Anyone who believes "we are going to win the war on terrorism" must be living on a different planet than me. I have spent almost my entire career in anti terrorist activity, and, in the whole of that time, only one of the many terrorist organizations was "defeated" by forceful confrontation. (The Bader-Meinhoff Gang which had been terrorizing Germany in the 1970's was rounded up after years of intense police activity. Yet even after the original gang was imprisoned where they committed suicide, it was a further 15 years before the reign of terror by their followers in the Red Army ceased.) In nearly all other instances of cessation of terrorist activities, these came after the particular terrorist organization had become redundant, or support for the organization dwindled in the population at large. The attempt to defeat the Islamic extremist terrorist movement by force has resulted in tens of thousands of additional terrorists joining the asymmetric fight against the forces of democracy. The Israeli government has been fighting a "war" on terrorism since the formation of the country. They have expended great efforts and many lives in this fight. They have responded to each terrorist atrocity in the same way, delivering death and destruction to the enemy, hoping that this time it will have a better result than the last. The result of this retaliation policy is that their most feared terrorist organization, Hamas is now in government in Gaza, and the standing of Hezbollah in the Arab community has never been higher. We in the US seem to be taking the failed Israeli model of retaliation as the answer to our own terrorist threats. This policy is having entirely the opposite effect to that which is desired, and terrorist incidents continue to escalate as thousands of our troops continue to be targeted. This, in-your-face confrontation of terrorist activity, polarizes non involved members of the population causing an escalation of the problem. The international escalation of radical Islamic terrorist incidents has, since the Iraq war, extended to countries such as England, Denmark, Holland and India. What we need are more innovative approaches to this pressing problem, and perhaps there are some lessons we can learn from more successful campaigns carried out in the past two thousand years.

The Flattening World

The trend in globalization of business and the flattening effect of the internet are combining to export fungible jobs to areas of lower paid labor. None of the western democracies have found a workable answer to this trend and many are suffering high unemployment rates. In March 2006, unemployment in Germany reached 5.2 million which represented 12.6% of the working age population. This is the highest rate since the 1930's and was greeted with a headline in the popular tabloid, Bild, pleading "Do Something". Politicians in the Western Democracies have been either slow or impotent to provide an answer to this trend. Unfortunately the "Something" might mean rolling back the development of the Social Democracy until a new direction can be found which will be viable in the 21st century. One obvious initiative which would help is for labor to become more mobile, i.e. be able to move from jobs in decline to those in demand. This inevitably means that the labor force will need to be better educated initially (in school), and more easily re-educated to perform more technical jobs. Unfortunately just when we need students who are better educated, the standard of achievement has gone down. The National Assessment of Educational Progress, otherwise known as the "national report card" in America, reported that twelfth graders in 2006 performed worse in reading than in 1992. Only 35% of students were proficient in reading and 23% were proficient in mathematics. This sorry state does not bode well for our ability to thrive in the flat world where Asian students are matriculating in ever greater numbers, and where in 2007, March Tian Boedihardjo, a nine year old student, was enrolled on a mathematics course at the Hong Kong Baptist University.

The impact on labor of flattening the World has not yet been fully felt in the US since we have been able to persuade foreign exporters of goods and materials into the States to reinvest the proceeds back into the US economy. In the mid nineties, the German company, BMW, opened a manufacturing plant in Spartanburg South Carolina from where it now supplies the world demand for all roadsters and sports activity vehicles. Clearly there is something seriously wrong with German labor laws and practices to cause good companies like BMW to abandon their base where arguably the best engineers in the world reside. The labor market in the US on the other hand has been pegged at the bottom end by 11 million illegal immigrants who are without a legal franchise to demand better wages and conditions of employment. This factor has kept industrial and agricultural costs in check, but is this a good foundation on which the greatest democracy in the World should rely?

Illegal Immigration

Illegal immigration is an issue which has received ambivalent attention from both our political leaders and security forces. New initiatives have been proposed to build a high wall across the southern border of The United States which undoubtedly will slow the flow of illegal immigrants. Unfortunately, because there is such a discrepancy of job availability and wage differential, the pressure to find work in the US is so great, that immigrants will continue to overcome such futile attempts to close the border. There is a similar stream of illegal immigrants into the United Kingdom, but none, to my knowledge, have entered by swimming the Channel.

The higher paid sector of society in the US benefits greatly from the large pool of cheap illegal labor. We all enjoy cheap food and services such as cleaning and landscaping that are staffed with a high proportion of immigrants. So why is illegal immigration such a major problem? Some industries such as the meat packing industry have thrived on illegal or new immigrants for over one hundred years. The Bureau of Citizenship and Immigration Services estimates that 25% of the meat processing workforce in Nebraska and Iowa are working with false documents. Cleaning crews in the packing industry are almost all new or illegal immigrants. The great shame is that these people are treated almost as badly as the slaves of the nineteenth century. Jeremy Olson, a reporter with the Omaha World Herald estimated that in the period since 1987, thirty people had died and hundreds more were injured in meat packinghouse cleaning incidents. How can the Law adequately protect these people who are themselves illegal? Also, by accepting people in our midst who are here illegally, we corrupt the respect for the rule of law which inevitably leads to further lawlessness.

Loss of Credibility of Financial Institutions

The capitalist system of open competition in free markets is now under considerable threat because of the collapse of trust between financial institutions brought about by the failure of so many sub-prime mortgages. The enormous volume of bad debt caused by so many failures has not only created an illiquid situation which has drained the life-blood from our capitalist society, but has also created a total lack of confidence and credibility between banks and financial institutions since nobody trusts the validity of the information on balance sheets which may be affected by the toxic debt. Confidence is at the root of capitalist society, and without it, bankers will not make loans, and none of the captains of industry will invest in new products and processes which are essential to produce growth in the economy. We can only hope that world governments learned enough from the trials of the great depression to be able to steer us out of the present catastrophe. There have already been many television programs and newspaper articles pointing fingers and apportioning blame, and I will not add to those other than to point out that self regulation of our financial institutions has not worked to prevent this disaster, and imposition of government control will herald many of the worst features of communist ideology which has also been shown to be a failure. We must therefore seek new innovative methods of automatic control of all financial institutions which will return confidence to the validity of information on income statements and balance sheets of all companies and financial institutions.

The Chronic Trade Imbalance

Perhaps the most serious issue which is not acknowledged by many in the Executive Branch or even in the financial community in the U.S. is the chronic imbalance of trade with the rest of the World. This is a classic example of the "not broke, don't fix it" principle. In the US, both exports and imports have been rising for many years. During the sixties, the trade balance of the US with the rest of the World was positive in every year. However, the US has had a negative trade balance with the rest of the World for goods and services in every year since 1976. During the late nineties and through the first part of the twenty first century, the trade imbalance has increased at an alarming rate, reaching $723 billion in 2005. Under normal conditions, the balancing forces of supply and demand would cause depreciation of the currency, as there would be more sellers than buyers of the currency. This would be a good example of a self-regulating system, for as the currency depreciates, home goods are more competitive and exports increase to balance the imports. In any other country in the World, such a serious imbalance of trade would however have resulted in the collapse of that country's currency, producing a situation such as occurred in Germany in 1923, when German workers took their weekly wage home in wheelbarrows. The major difference between the dollar and all other currencies is that for almost a century, the dollar has been used as the currency of choice between nations when trading with one another. Today, oil is traded in dollars between nations independent of the U.S. The excess dollars earned by countries exporting to the U.S. are either used in international trade or to buy U.S. assets and bonds. Thomas Jefferson, who disliked the whole idea of a Federal Bank made a comment to John Taylor in a letter of 1816: "I sincerely believe . . . . that the principle of spending money to be paid by posterity under the name of funding is but swindling futurity on a large scale" In early 2006, foreign entities owned a little more than 53% of the U.S. federal debt (approximately $2 trillion) purchased in publicly traded world markets. The value of the income stream from US owned assets abroad is now, for the first time in modern history, below the value of the interest paid to foreign creditors. Shares in U.S. companies are also a favorite target of foreign investors with dollars to spend. The organization, Economy in Crisis, claims that whole industries are now controlled by foreign interests, particularly the important opinion-influencing industries such as movie making and book publishing which are more than 60% foreign owned. This process of foreign acquisition came to attention of the public at large in April

2006 when one of the oil rich Sheikdoms of the Gulf made a bid to buy control of a company which included US Ports. There were serious concerns for the security of the ports and the proposal was opposed in the Senate.

The use of the dollar as an international currency has been an important aid to stimulating international commerce. It is all the more important therefore to exercise the fiscal responsibility necessary to maintain the stability and value of the dollar. To continue to accept trade deficits approaching a trillion dollars is extremely irresponsible, it taxes our children and grandchildren, it makes American business vulnerable to foreign buyers with dollars to spend, and when we run out of assets to sell, it will eventually lead to economic collapse. Successive governments seem to have been impotent in tackling this problem, but new Gaian type of self regulatory processes will be explored here which will ensure a better balance of trade, and should not be painful to implement.

The Law

In the US, no other part of society is in such need for urgent change as the system of law. The system of justice in America, long envied by many suppressed peoples around the World, has become an object of ridicule. The Law provides the ground rules for all social interactions between people and institutions. It has given successive generations of people and corporations confidence to feel safe in doing the right thing. Today however, the many instances of ridiculous litigation awards and jury verdicts are causing severe decline in several sectors of society, because people no longer feel safe doing what's right. I was first attracted to work in America in no small part by the enthusiastic "can do" attitude of American researchers, and suppliers. This attitude has unfortunately changed in some important areas of our lives. George McGovern and Alan K. Simpson in the April 17th 2002 edition of the Wall Street Journal wrote: "Up and down the levels of responsibility in schools, hospitals and courts, "can do" has been replaced with "can't do". Talk to teachers and doctors, and their frustration erupts. Teachers feel crushed by bureaucracy and no longer have authority to maintain order in classrooms. With doctors, the situation is worse. A new poll suggests that doctors, instead of focusing on the best medical judgment, worry more about protecting themselves from potential lawsuits." The spiraling cost of healthcare and the declining position of US education verses the rest of the World can be attributed in a large part to the failure of the legal system to continue to provide the necessary conditions for constructive relationships.

The rule of Law in western democracies has been the main instrument in ensuring our freedoms and giving confidence that in doing the "right things" in our lives, we would have the support of The Law. In England, a writ of Habeas Corpus has protected the right of individuals to a hearing before a Court of Law since the Anglo Saxon era at the end of the first millennium. It was already common law by the time the Magna Carta was signed in 1215 by the mediaeval tyrant, King John. It was confirmed in an act of the British parliament in 1679, and since then, has been adopted by the US, and has only been suspended in times of war. It has been used to ensure that detention of individuals by both authorities and other members of society, cannot continue without a hearing to examine the legality of the detention. Today, this long held "right" is being eroded by the governments of both the UK and USA in detaining terror suspects indefinitely. But this "right" is not one which occupies most American's thoughts as they go about their daily lives. A major concern which does occupy our daily thoughts is the fear of being sued in the course of our normal business and social activities. This fear is not unfounded, since in some States, the Law will support the right of even burglars to sue property owners if they get injured during their nefarious activities. Philip Howard wrote in his book, The Collapse of the Common Good, "Social relations in America, far from steadied by law's sure hand, are a tangle of frayed nerves. Any dealings in public—whether in hospitals, schools, offices, or in the ebb and flow of daily life—are fraught with legal anxiety. An undertow pulls at us constantly, drawing us away from choices that we believe are reasonable. Legal fear has become a defining feature of our culture." The old joke in the automotive industry alleged that if a Japanese car manufacturer has a problem with one of its products, it would hire another 1000 engineers to put it right. If a US manufacturer has a problem, it hires another 1000 lawyers. This is not so far away from reality, for in 1999, General Motors was found liable for $4.9 billion by a jury in Los Angeles for siting the fuel tank on its Chevy Malibu line too near the back bumper where it exploded in a rear end accident. The award, made to the family involved in the accident, was $107 million for pain and suffering and $4.8 billion in punitive damages. The jury was quick to make this decision after it learned that GM had determined it cost less to settle law suits from injuries and deaths in fuel fires than spend $8.59 to relocate the tank in each car. The size of this award is greater than the GDP of 28% of the countries in the World! Clearly, US industry cannot stay in business long when awards of this size are made. One series of law suits against Merck relating to their Viox product was predicted by some to cost the company in excess of $20 billion. This was well above the value of the stockholder's equity on the balance sheet, and could have forced the company into bankruptcy, thereby denying the public at large the possible benefit of many research programs being conducted in Merck. The shareholders of a company levied with punitive damages are not guilty of any offense, but they certainly pay the price of management's willful negligence, since no insurance covers punitive damages. Sarbanes-Oxley goes some way toward making management more responsible for what goes on in their company, but this does not extend too far beyond the normal fiscal responsibilities which they should, and most do, rigorously exercise. Boards of Directors which represent the interest of shareholders are mostly not competent to determine the product liability risks in the company, or management's attention to those risks. They abrogate responsibility many times to government bodies such as the FDA or NRC, who themselves are insulated from suit and cannot compel companies to release all files on their products. We need a paradigm shift in how responsibility is exercised at the same time as awards are made more realistic. What happened to the principle of similar cases being decided alike? We also need a paradigm shift in the attitude of both the public at large and our politicians who are content to let individual lawsuits determine the safety of our products, our infrastructure, and our lives. I am sure that most of the families of victims hurt by products, or negligence on the part of individuals, would prefer to have their loved ones alive and healthy rather than become rich from their unfortunate condition or death.

The most insidious effect of litigation is that the law is now not only failing to provide those freedoms that we desire, but is acting against the common good. The fear of suit, for example, is not working to make childbirth safer. It is forcing more doctors out of gynecology and making pre and post natal care beyond the budget of many Americans. Scott B Ransom and associates from the Department of Obstetrics and Gynecology at the University of Michigan Medical School reported in the June, 2005 issue of Obstetrics and Gynecology that "everybody wants a perfect baby, leading many people to sue when the reality doesn't match their expectation." The Michigan University research showed that malpractice insurance premiums vary widely from state to state, Florida being the highest premium state with average 2004 premiums exceeding $195,000. Major metropolitan areas in Florida have the highest premiums and also the highest rate of increase. Between 2003 and 2004, Dade County annual premiums went from $249,000 to $277,000. Such exorbitant premiums pushes the cost of gynecological services beyond the means of poorer American mothers and allows even greater awards at litigation, thus producing a continuing spiral of health cost. Many experienced GYN doctors are leaving the field, so that in addition to the increased cost, there is also a reduction relative to other developed nations in the quality of care. The cost of healthcare in the US is roughly twice that of the United Kingdom for example, and the infant mortality rate of 6.63 deaths per 1000 live births is almost twice that of the top 10 countries in the World, placing the US in 36th position in World ranking. The US has arguably the best medical equipment in the world and doctors who rate among the best in the World, so we must conclude that it is the health system which is broken and needs fixing. This will be impossible however without first "fixing" the legal system which is getting in the way of progress. There are several initiatives and pressure groups which are attempting to encourage change in the American legal system. Groups such as The Common Good have recruited some influential members of Congress to press for legislative changes which should nibble away at the problem, but while ever Congress is comprised of a majority of lawyers, I fear that "The Common Good" will be relegated to a lower level of importance than that given to the maintenance of the existing rule of law, and the status of lawyers in our community.

The Environment

High on the list of problems which we need to solve is our impact on the environment. There are many who believe that society should manage various aspects of our environment for the greater benefit of its inhabitants. Unfortunately our record of achievement in many areas of environmental management has been well below that which may have been intended or desired. Projects such as the early management of Yellowstone Park have been lessons in how not to approach environmental management. Alston Chase, in his book "Playing God In Yellowstone" shows how good intentions by environmentalists upset the natural balance of nature. Once man had interfered with this balance, it forced more and more intervention in order to prevent total disaster. The lessons learned from such mistakes must now be applied to the much more important issues of man's impact on the World environment. There is now almost unanimous agreement in the scientific community that Global Warming is increasing at an unprecedented pace. It may already be unstoppable until it results in the melting of the polar ice caps and the destruction of much of life on Earth. Evidence of the link between global warming and the level of CO2 in the atmosphere is historically very convincing. We must not however be lead into the trap of trying to control the global environment, all we can do is to ensure that man does not poison Gaia, and destroy **her** ability to maintain control. It is of the utmost urgency that new international controls are put in place to ensure that Gaia can remain in control of the many essential environmental parameters, so that our grandchildren and their grandchildren can enjoy her many bounties.

Government Negligence

All the issues detailed here serve to indicate that the very fabric of U.S. government at all levels of Federal, State and local is failing and in need of urgent change. Politicians and civil servants alike have become unaccountable and unwilling to take responsibility to improve their performance in governorship. Twelve million illegal aliens are here because Government allows them to be here illegally. Even illegal aliens who have been convicted of multiple crimes have not been expelled. Government has got much worse at a time when industry and commerce have been impelled by the forces of open competition to embrace policies of continuous improvement. There are many examples of government failure and ineptitude, but the one foremost in people's mind is probably the response of the Federal Emergency Management Agency to the damage caused by hurricane Katrina. The Red Cross and Salvation Army were much quicker to respond than our Government which has much greater resources. Another failure was recently highlighted by the way government took control of the Iraq economy. Anyone with a computer connection to the internet can, in a fraction of a second find almost any item of information which may be desired. We can check our bank balance from thousands of miles away in almost any foreign country, but our government chose to ship 360 tons of $100 dollar bills into a war zone to pay for the reconstruction of Iraq. It is no surprise that $8.8 billion remains unaccounted for, but who is held accountable? Even Newt Gingrich, former Speaker of the House of Representatives, now recognizes in his book "Real Change" that "Our system of government is on a course of decline and disaster. The system won't deliver the change we need." I believe the change we need more than any other is for our government to govern with responsibility, accountability and efficiency.

We do not need new laws to get DUI drivers off our roads. We do not need new laws to send home convicted criminal illegal aliens. We do not need new laws to prevent fraudulent welfare claims. We do not need new laws to get guns out of the hands of convicted criminals. We do not need new laws to improve the standard of education in our schools. We do not need new laws to prevent fraudulent issue of social security cards. We **do** need new laws to find better ways to make government attend to the job of governing, and ensure that the resourceful people of America are no longer penalized for doing the right thing.

Chapter 2

Cybernetic Social Systems

Cybernetics is defined in Webster's dictionary as the science of communication and control theory that is concerned especially with the comparative study of automatic control systems. The science has been developed to a level where only competent mathematicians with powerful computers can contribute further. I do not count myself as one of this elite community, but I do understand sufficient to bring the non scientists into meaningful discussion on how cybernetics can be applied to social systems. Consider a common control system such as the central heating system in ones home. The essential elements of the system are the energy supply, (either a gas burner or electrical heater), a means of conveying the energy into the room (hot air or hot water in radiators) a temperature sensor, and a control system that incorporates a required temperature setting. Some control systems regulate the amount of heat into the room depending on the difference between the set point and the actual temperature in the room. This is known as proportional control. When the temperature control system is first switched on, and the temperature is well below the set point, maximum available heating is applied, and the temperature rises to a point where proportional control kicks in and power is gradually reduced. The band of temperature over which this occurs is known as the proportional band. If the proportional band is small then the gain in the control loop is said to be high. On the other hand, if the proportional band is large then the gain is low. The advantage of high gain in a control system is that the set point may be more accurately achieved, and is reached more quickly, since maximum power is maintained for the longest time. Unfortunately, there is always a lag between the temperature of the room air and the thermometer in the control system, so that when the temperature reaches the set point and the heating is switched off, the temperature of at least part of the room continues to rise above the set point. After a while, with no more heat entering the room, the temperature falls back below the set point and heat is again applied. If the gain of the control system is high, and the lag between the actual and measured temperatures too great, the temperature will continue to oscillate and will never reach a steady state. Oscillation is a common phenomenon in control systems and can be a sure indication that closed loop control is being applied. For example, when studying the temperature of the earth over the last million years or so, the ice ages and interglacial periods have a strong resemblance to oscillations produced by a system under control. The period of oscillation has been remarkably constant at about 100,000 years for the last 500,000 years. Oscillation in a control system is most often overcome by reducing the gain of the system. Under these conditions, the set point is approached more slowly and the temperature eventually reaches a steady state. The temperature of the steady state is not quite at the set point however, since there must always be a difference, or error, to cause heat to be supplied. The higher the gain in the system, the closer will be the actual temperature to the desired set point, but the system will be more prone to oscillation.

More sophisticated systems rely on the measurement of more parameters than the differential between actual and desired temperature. For example proportional, integral and derivative controls (P.I.D.) will measure both the length of time away from the set point and the rate of change of temperature and apply a computer algorithm to achieve a more accurate result. These systems, sometimes known as three term controls, can accommodate larger and faster fluctuations of external conditions than can a simple proportional control system, and can remain in stable control. The temperature of such systems can also be more quickly changed without losing control. A further parameter, sometimes known as predictive control, can be added into a control system which is already under PID control. I will illustrate this in an application for controlling high tech instrumentation ovens. These ovens are typically heated by an electric heating element and the power is controlled in a control loop which determines the proportion of the available power to apply in order to maintain the temperature very accurately. Suppose one such oven is under control and demanding 50% available power. If suddenly the voltage of the power supply fell 5%, then this would be detected as a fall in temperature after the time lag in the system. The control system would act to bring it back into control at the desired set point but not until a perturbation of the temperature had occurred. It is much better to have a predictive control which monitors the voltage of the supply and changes the demanded proportion of the available power to compensate. In this case the proportion of the available power would be increased by 10%, since the power is proportional to the square of the voltage. This type of predictive control could be very useful in controlling economies where time lags in the system can be many months and sometimes years before the effect of an external change is detected in economic performance.

The design and sighting of the sensing thermometer in the system is extremely important. It needs to be of low thermal inertia to respond quickly to changes and should not be too near or too far away from the heat input. Consider a thermostat that is intimately attached to the north wall of the room which is being controlled. The temperature which is being sensed is not the room temperature, but the wall temperature which may be several degrees below the room temperature, and severely affected by outside temperature fluctuations. If the set point remains constant in this system throughout the year, the controller will attempt to maintain the wall temperature constant throughout the seasons. In winter, this will take much more heat and the room temperature will inevitably rise well above the set point in order to achieve this. Such a system would be said to achieve a negative steady state error, i.e. the colder it is outside, the warmer it gets inside.

The application of a control system to control the temperature of our homes is only one example of many control systems used in technology to control temperature, flowrates, pressures, levels of liquid, automatic speed controls etc. All these have been remarkably successful in achieving a desired result. Why then have the same principles of control not been applied to society in general? The simple answer is that several types of feedback control are indeed exercised in our society. One example of a control system is in the way governments attempt to control economic activity. Governments seek to improve the standard of living by encouraging growth of the gross domestic product in a controlled way. The "fuel" in this control system is money. Insufficient money supply inhibits investment and growth. A surfeit of money produces inflationary pressures and encourages bad investment, ultimately causing bankruptcies such as occurred during the Savings and Loan debacle in the 1980's, and the more recent problem caused by the failure of many sub-prime mortgages. The foot on the regulator pedal for this control in each western democracy belongs to the central bank. The US Federal Reserve Bank or the FED as it is more commonly known, attempts to exercise control of the money supply through the Federal Open Market Committee, by adjusting short term interest rates, and buying and selling

Treasury paper. The rational for this is fully explained in Martin Mayer's book, The FED, which I would recommend to all who wish to understand more fully the mechanisms involved in control of the economy. When the controls were first exercised, banks were the major suppliers of financing to American commerce and industry, so that any restrictions placed on the banks by the FED showed up quickly in reduced economic activity. Like many control systems with long time lags, the economy hovers in a continual state of instability. The resulting changes in GDP as measured by the U.S. Department of Commerce show cycles of economic activity with periods of expansion followed by periods of recession. These economic cycles during the 19th and most of the 20th century occurred fairly regularly with a duration of about four years.

The parameter which is traditionally measured by the central bankers to decide whether to use the accelerator or the brake is some measure of inflation. Historically, high inflation levels have resulted from an easy money supply. A small amount of inflation is regarded to be beneficial, so that there is a strong incentive to put capital to work. Some positive value of inflation may be targeted, such as is employed by the newly independent Bank of England. Unfortunately this is not an easy parameter to measure, nor does it differentiate between domestic causes and those caused by external circumstances. Attempting to cure inflation caused by external forces such as the escalating price of imported oil by putting the brakes on the domestic economy only gives rise to dreaded stagflation. In this case, inflation is not caused by excessive money supply, and reducing the money supply will compound the problem and may lead to recession. Also the inertia in economies ensures that when high inflation is detected, applying the brakes will not immediately bring inflation under control, but instead causes the economy to swing from expansion to contraction. The loop gain and the time lag in the control system in such cases are often too great to achieve a steady state of growth without employing sophisticated control algorithms with many inputs to measure money supply and other factors such as rate of change of inflation. External changes, some of which can be very rapid such as declaration of war, the collapse of a trading partner's economy or currency, or as occurred recently, liquidity is suddenly reduced by a rash of house foreclosures, can cause loss of control, sending the economy into a nose dive. In such circumstances, it would be advisable to apply predictive control inputs and not wait until the external change causes the economy to take a nose dive. Fortunately, in the U.S. we had a magician at the controls during the past fifteen years or so who anticipated changes before they were detected, and understood the need for paying attention to more inputs than a simple measure of inflation. Mr. Alan Greenspan also can be credited with reducing the gain in the control loop to match the response time of the economy. In the early 90's, I remember reading an article in the financial press which accused the FED Chairman of "tinkering" with interest rates after a number of quarter point changes had been made over several months, when the author thought a bigger change was required. Moving the interest rate in small steps had the same effect as reducing the loop gain in the example of the domestic temperature control system, and enabled stable conditions of economic expansion in the last decade of the twentieth century for the longest period on record of over ten years. An optimum rate of interest for that time was approached slowly, and became known as the soft landing. Control engineers would call it critically damped.

This example of control of the economy is a classic case of a negative feedback control loop, the system responds to changes in measured inflation/deflation rates by adjusting money supply in the opposite direction to the inflation or deflation, thus maintaining a low inflation rate and, hopefully, an increasing GDP. This is still not an automatic control system however, since the decision making is taken by a human element. We may not be so lucky in the future to have such competent members of the Federal Open Market Committee with their hands on the controls. It will be beneficial to have a more stable system for control of economic activity which will work automatically, in a similar way to the operation of automatic landing systems used in commercial airliners, where the captain can take over at any time. It may, however, be some years before we have sufficiently reliable input data and control algorithms to allow totally "hands off" operation of the economy at large. The present system of control also has an inherent flaw in that the parameter which needs to be controlled, i.e. the money supply is not measured in the control loop. What is measured is a parameter which is affected by the money supply. But this parameter, inflation, might also be affected by other external influences. I will liken this to trying to control a room temperature by monitoring the skin temperature of a naked man within the room. Most of the time, this will work adequately to provide a comfortable environment. Unfortunately, the skin temperature is also dependent on what is going on inside the body of the man. If he participates in aerobic exercise, or if he becomes ill and runs a fever, then his own core body temperature will rise and his skin temperature will also rise. The control system would detect this and shut down the heat supply to the room which would produce dire conditions for the subject. I am not suggesting that the existing system of control of the economy will result in total collapse, but it has resulted in some scary moments including the present crisis of liquidity and confidence caused by the failure of the banking system to control its own operations adequately.

In the capitalist system of free market competition, hitherto, only government regulation and self imposed controls have been relied on to provide the necessary environment for healthy competition. Unfortunately, as society has become more complex and fast moving, more wide boys and crooks have taken over some of the once proud financial institutions and have manipulated the system in their own short term favor without any consideration of the long term health of the banking system or the economy in general. This has been like the baseball players who took steroids to gain a competitive advantage, but failed to see that they were killing both themselves and their sport. The debacle caused by the collapse of several major banking corporations, will inevitably lead to more government regulations and control as Congress seeks to protect the people's investment in the various financial institutions. The financial institutions have shown that they cannot regulate themselves, but is increased government control really the only other answer? Self imposed controls in a competitive environment are not the answer since each individual will always seek to get a competitive advantage, or manipulate the system to his/her advantage. Consider a large auditorium or meeting room in which there is open access to the heating or cooling supply to the room. Eskimos, Amazonian Indians and New Yorkers in the room would continually be adjusting the supply for their own comfort level and as a result, nobody would be satisfied. Many years ago, I had the privilege to supply explosives detection equipment to the Houses of Parliament in London, during which time I discovered that the heating and cooling of the House of Commons was controlled by the facility manager who observed the Members through a periscope from the bowels of the building. If they appeared to be perspiring or loosening their ties, he would reduce the heating manually. Government control of financial institutions is analogous to, and as antiquated as the manual control of that system of heating in the Houses of parliament. It will be much better to eliminate both self control systems and government controls and devise automatic control systems that can be set up and defined by government legislation, but operated by employees of the organization in a quality system such as that defined by the ISO 9000 standard, where responsibilities are rigorously defined for everyone in the system. Traceability and accuracy of data will be improved since emphasis is placed on getting it right first time rather than relying on the audit process which is often superficial as was the case in Enron. Rewards can be made to individuals based on both their own and company performance to provide the necessary feedback mechanism of rewarding good performance and penalizing bad performance. A.L. Williams, a successful life insurance company, rewarded its sales members based on the volume of sales brought in during the period. However, if the insurance was not continued into subsequent years, the bonus was clawed back. If this system of reward had been operated in the mortgage industry, I am sure that many of the problems of toxic debt would never have arisen.

Many of society's challenges will not unfortunately be helped by the application of classical negative feedback control systems to provide desired results. The principle of negative feedback is nevertheless very sound, where desired behavior is rewarded and undesired behavior penalized. This principle is employed by nature in ensuring a balance between many coexisting species. Jim Lovelock in his book Gaia detailed his hypothesis that life on Earth works in concert to regulate and maintain the conditions most comfortable for the continued health of life on the planet. It was natural that many scientists and laymen would find this hypothesis hard to swallow, for how could so many disparate life forms (plants, animals, insects, bacteria, etc) work in concert when they cannot even communicate with one another? Also, what would be the sensing mechanisms employed by such a large scale system? In order to explain how this can occur, Jim later related the now famous parable of daisyworld, (Watson and Lovelock 1983) to demonstrate that a self regulating system would transpire from the physically intimate coupling between life and its material environment without conscious intent or planning (teleology).

Daisyworld as described by Lovelock and Watson is a hypothetical planet inhabited by white daisies and black daisies. The planet is warmed by a sun of varying luminosity. The planet receives increased radiation over time as the sun warms up, but at first, in the cool period, the black daisies thrive by absorbing a larger proportion of radiation and warm the environment thus allowing some white daisies to grow. The white daisies reflect more of the sunlight and act to cool the planet. As the solar luminosity increases the white daisies gradually take over and predominate. Lovelock and Watson showed that while there were both types of daisy on the planet the temperature would remain steady over a range that would warm a bare planet by over 60 degree centigrade. They also showed that the temperature of the planet would cool slightly as the sun brightens, i.e. it would achieve a negative steady state error. In a later refinement, Lovelock described a system (Lovelock 1992) which included many types of daisy, herbivores (rabbits) and carnivores (foxes). Such a system shows remarkable stability and can accommodate fluctuations of the populations of species and still remain stable. It shows that the greater the diversification of species, the more stable the system becomes.

The discovery of such a self regulating system has prompted a whole new field of control theory and has now been accredited with the maintenance of stable conditions in other physiological control situations (Saunders et al., 1998 and Koeslag et al., 1999). It may be rewarding to consider the possible application of Daisyworld control in some social situations. After all, the party political system of government is itself a daisyworld system with two competing parties in the same space. We can also explore how increased stability can be achieved by allowing more contributors to compete in the same space.

Just to get started on this quest, I will relate an actual example of traffic flow in an offset junction of four roads in Cambridge England. (Remember, the Brits travel on the left side of the road). The main road was the old London to Cambridge road which ran straight into the city, and the other road crossed this with an offset of about 50 meters forming two T junctions.

In the early days of motorized vehicles, no controls were applied and the traffic entering the city on the London road claimed the right of way, causing traffic to build up unacceptably each morning along the route coming into the city from the west. Clearly this was an unacceptable situation and soon traffic lights were mounted on the two junctions to alleviate the problem. Unfortunately as levels of traffic increased over time, the short road between the junctions became jammed on a morning when the lights were red. Traffic was only allowed through the junction in short slugs since when the lights were green at the first light they were frequently red at the second. The result was that fewer vehicles were now able to transit through the junctions than before. The only consolation was that both traffic flows felt the pain equally. Filter lights and computer control of the two junctions were attempted but still traffic hold ups continued since flow through the junctions was periodically halted as the lights changed, and traffic patterns varied throughout the day and seasons. Finally, the lights were taken out and two white spots approximately a meter across were painted in the middle of each junction to form two mini rotaries (roundabouts). At a stroke, the worst of the traffic nightmare was eliminated. What happened was that the decision was given to each motorist to determine whether it was safe to pass through the junction. In order to allow this decision, it is essential that all drivers know and obey the rules of using any rotary. All drivers approaching a rotary must yield to those already in the rotary, and the speed through the rotary is such that will allow those entering to fit into gaps in the traffic. This system worked well during the time I lived in Cambridge, but of course will not work at all levels of traffic density. The essential message here is that better regulation is achieved when decision making is given to more of the people involved in a situation structured to allow such decisions. Most people would recognize a set of traffic lights as forming a control system, but the better control system in this case is provided by the members of society who use it.

Most man made cybernetic social systems, however, will most frequently be of the proportional control type in which parameters are measured to determine the effect of the applied changes or practices, so that feedback is obtained on the efficacy of the changes imposed. The change can then be either reinforced or reduced depending on the results which are measured. One of the best recent examples of this is the way which Mayor Giuliani and New York City police chief Bill Bratton set about reducing crime in the City. Bratton realized that before improvements could be made, metrics would be needed to chart the progress or lack thereof. His drive for more informative metrics upset many of the precinct captains who refused to divert officer's time off the beat and onto a computer, where they were asked to collate data on crime in the precinct. The exercise however proved very effective and allowed Chief Bratton to align his forces more effectively against the criminals and achieve a 50% reduction in the murder rate in the city. I believe that many more of our social systems will improve when subjected to the measured effects of change.

Chapter 3

Avoiding Positive Feedback

We have seen in the last chapter how negative feedback control can produce a stable, regulated system despite changes in external influences. It is easy to see what might happen in a control loop with positive feedback, for if the sensor determined it was too hot, the system would provide more heat, thereby producing a runaway situation. In Daisy World terms, this would be as if the white daisies thrived better in cold conditions and the black daisies thrived only in hot conditions. The temperature of the environment would never be stabilized since only white daisies would thrive initially which would then reduce the temperature further making the environment unsuitable for either species. No control engineer would make the mistake of designing a system which would immediately loose control. Why then do our political leaders devise systems with the best intensions, but with no regard to the positive feedback effects resulting from their actions? Often the results of legislation produce the exact opposite effect to that which is desired. Nowhere is this more evident than in social services and welfare payment practices. Before the welfare reform law of Aug 1996, cash assistance was made to needy families from the Federal Government under Aid to Families with Dependent Children (AFDC). Nearly all the payments were made to unmarried mothers, and were a positive disincentive for recipients to marry, since each family was means tested for family income. Payments under the AFDC scheme were counter productive in helping families escape from poverty, and for several decades relentless increases in the proportion of births to unmarried mothers were recorded. Some of the incentive to remain on welfare was reduced by the 1996 welfare reform act, when the responsibility was handed to the States under the Temporary Assistance to

Needy Families (TANF) scheme. Since then, welfare rolls have dropped dramatically. The proportion of births to unmarried mothers has, however remained stubbornly steady at around 33%. The benefits of growing up with two biological parents are widely acknowledged, and both the Bush Administration and Congress sought legislative ways to encourage this. Still, many States give preference to single parent families in allocating child care and housing subsidies. Also all welfare is income tested which creates an incentive for fathers with earnings and mothers without earnings to live apart or feign such separation. Children who grow up in this poverty trap with a single parent account for 72% of teenage murders, 60% of rape crimes and are 11 times more likely to exhibit violent behavior. Not only do they do less well in school, high concentrations of children from single parent families have a detrimental effect on the performance of other children in the school who are from two parent families. The result of the legislation is that children from single parent families will be less likely to escape the poverty trap and will provide more candidates for welfare in their adulthood.

In the late 90's I had occasion to make a business trip to Cairo, Egypt. The company I visited was in the centre of town in a drab office building in a street of similar buildings which had not had a coat of paint in the previous 40 years or so. The elevator in the lobby looked like one from a 1930's movie with steel mesh doors. Its speed was such that one could easily beat it to the third floor by using the staircase. My associate apologized for the dilapidated state of the building and explained that there had been a city ordinance for many years which prevented landlords increasing the rents. As a result, they were unable to afford the maintenance costs. Rather than encourage more industry to thrive in the city, this ordinance had forced several companies to move out of the city to the more modern offices in the suburb of Giza where they have encroached on the only wonder of the ancient world still standing.

Another similar case of positive feedback achieving the opposite effect to that which was desired was the so called Rachman legislation in England. The Tory Government of 1957 attempted to speed the rebuilding of London, still blighted by bomb damage, by relaxing all rent controls. This produced a situation in which slum landlords were able to charge extortionate rents particularly to immigrants. The worst excesses were committed by the slum landlord, Rachman. So great were his extortionate activities that the practice became known as Rachmanism. When the Labor Party came to power in 1964, they legislated to again regulate rents and rental contract conditions. The effect of the new regulations was that many rental properties were taken off the market. Neither of these legislated situations yielded the desired result, but won votes in their relevant constituencies.

It is not always legislation which causes unwanted positive feedback, policies and tactics adopted by Federal, State and local governments can have even greater impact from positive feedback. There has been much debate as to why America went to war with Sadam Hussein's administration, but at the time, most people in the U.S. believed that it was a continuing effort in the so called war on terrorism. Sadam had indeed been sheltering the aging terrorist psychopath, Abu Nidal, of PLO and Black September fame, but Sadam had kept him under control. It is widely believed that he ordered Nidal's execution in 2002 well before the war started. Also, Osama bin Laden had no regard for Sadam, for on the 11th Feb 2003, a taped message from bin Laden was aired on al Jazeera TV describing Sadam as an infidel. At the time war began, there was only one small enclave of terrorist activity, and that was outside the Iraqi government control on the border with Iran. After the liberation, there are now tens of thousands of actual and potential radical Islamic terrorists in Iraq and many more have been recruited in other countries around the world. International terrorism has certainly been stimulated by the continued presence of U.S. troops in Iraq, and previously "quiet" countries such as India are now experiencing increased problems. This is the opposite result that most U.S. citizens expected to ensue from all the effort and sacrifices many have expended in their genuine desire to bring a better life to Iraq's people. To those more familiar with terrorist organizations and activities, however, the increase in terrorist activity comes as no surprise, and was entirely predictable. Foreign troops employed to quell unrest have always been the focus of the mob's violence, whether it be in Boston Massachusetts in 1773 or in Belfast in 1970, or in Iraq in 2006.

What lessons can we learn from these mistakes and ensure that we can do better in future? The first thing everyone involved in government must realize is that all social change impacts intelligent people who will invariably respond to the change in an attempt to protect or improve their own self interest. It seems that the political party in opposition cannot be relied on to argue the case for caution (case in point is the war in Iraq) so perhaps another body should be employed to determine possible positive feedback effects. Proposals for legislative and policy change could be vetted by some non partisan organization before it is allowed to be voted into law. Such an organization (The Economic Cybernetic Commission?) should be a statutory, possibly non-governmental, body in order to ensure honest analysis. (We have hitherto been ill served by organizations such as the CIA who the American Public had every right to believe to be apolitical in its analyses and reports, when in fact these have been given a spin by political masters to provide support for actions which had already been considered by the Government.) The U.S. Government Accountability Office (GAO) or the Law Commission for England and Wales for example, would be suitable homes for such bodies. It should be arranged so that they could co-opt outside expertise in specialist fields for each project. The Law Commission for England and Wales was created by the Law Commissions Act 1965 "to promote the reform of the law". This body is bound by statute to receive and consider any proposals for the reform of the law which are made or referred to the Commission. Most proposals for change come from Government Ministers or Departments, and there is a Ministerial Committee on the Law Commission which assists the process. The Law Commission has no expertise outside the legal and legislative areas, and new statutes would have to be enacted to extend their responsibility and expertise. The GAO in the US on the other hand, is a highly competent body that could easily take on responsibility of reporting on the likely economic and political feedback effects of policy or legislative changes.

There are some precedents for such advisory bodies, for example, the Vice Presidents Commission on Aviation Safety and Security was established by executive order of President Clinton in Aug. 1996. This ad hoc commission was composed of department heads from Government Agencies, industry leaders, security experts and a concerned member of the public. Even though many of the recommendations were taken from an earlier report to the Federal Aviation Administration, of the Baseline Working Group, it still took a year and a half to produce the final report. One would expect that a permanent commission with authority to co-opt specialists from industry and achedemia would become more efficient at bringing together the right experts to join permanent talent to examine each proposition. The Law Commission in the UK has been successful in ensuring that fewer mistakes are made by poor legislation, I see no reason a new body could not be equally successful in a more general way to mitigate the worst effects of unwanted and unforeseen positive feedback produced by legislative changes.

Chapter 4

Government and the Constitution

"The idea that institutions established for the use of the nation cannot be touched nor modified even to make them answer their end because of rights gratuitously supposed in those employed to manage them in trust for the public, may perhaps be a salutary provision against the abuses of a monarch but is most absurd against the nation itself. Yet our lawyers and priests generally inculcate this doctrine and suppose that preceding generations held the earth more freely than we do, had a right to impose laws on us unalterable by ourselves, and that we in like manner can make laws and impose burdens on future generations which they have no right to alter; in fine, that the earth belongs to the dead and not to the living."
Thomas Jefferson to William Plumer, 1816.

The US Constitution was originally drawn up to define how the individual States would relate and share power in a new central government. Each State was jealous of its independence and some had even been involved in armed conflict but without casualties. For example, Ethan Allan's Green Mountain Boys were a militia set up to resist the claims of New Yorkers on their lands in the New Hampshire Grants (later, Vermont). However, the thirteen States reluctantly gave up some of their previous powers in order to present a stronger posture on the international arena, and to better defend themselves against future attack especially from the British. However, even after the war of independence was won, the United States continued to be referred to in the plural. It was not until after the civil war that the singular version of The United States of America was adopted. Most countries in

1789 did not have a constitution, but the Preamble is a powerful statement of the motivation for a constitution, and is worth a reminder:

We the people of the United States, in Order to form a more perfect Union, establish Justice, insure domestic Tranquility, provide for the common defense, promote the general Welfare, and secure the Blessings of Liberty to ourselves and our Prosperity, do ordain and establish this Constitution for the United States of America.

Clearly the Founding Fathers planned to move towards a "more perfect Union", but the Union is much the same as it was in 1789. Although the other objectives still remain true today, much of the energy and drive of the early Americans has been eroded and replaced in part by cynicism, apathy, fear and greed. The recent demise, I believe, is caused by the failure to establish Justice, insure domestic Tranquility, and promote the general Welfare of the people. Is this somehow caused by recent changes in personal attitudes, or changes in the Law or interpretation of Constitutional clauses, or modern social and technological change? To investigate these possibilities, we must bear in mind that the tension between the largely agrarian Virginians and the more industrialized New Englanders and New Yorkers, was the stimulus for many of the clauses in the Constitution. The Federalists, led by Hamilton and Adams, wanted a strong central government whereas the Anti-Federalists, chiefly the Virginians, Jefferson and Madison, concerned for the preservation of their own lifestyle wanted to restrict the new government's powers, and guarantee liberties (not, incidentally, to their slaves or the Indians). The Bill of Rights was devised as an afterthought to make the terms of The Constitution more acceptable to the Anti-Federalists who opposed Big Government. The Bill of Rights was incorporated in the first ten Amendments, but these should be regarded as part of the original Constitution, since they were promised at the signing. The Bill of Rights largely confirmed that Natural Law, which was adapted from British Common Law, should decide individual's rights, and how they should relate to government and to one another. In 1798, just eleven years after the Constitution was signed, the US Supreme Court ruled that courts have the power to prevent legislatures from intruding upon natural rights because an act of any legislature contrary to the Natural Law cannot be considered a rightful exercise of legislative power. I like to think of the Natural Law as one would the second Law of Thermodynamics. They have both been given to us by God and there is no way of circumnavigating them. The Natural

Law, when practiced correctly, is a self regulating system and should not have caused the demise to which the country is headed. We will however consider the implications of changes in the practice of law in chapter 6. Let us first look at some of the fundamentals of our democracy as guaranteed by the Constitution to find out why it has become jaded, and sometimes held in cynical regard. Then perhaps we can begin to consider possible changes and improvements.

The first and second clauses of the Constitution allow for the election of Representatives by the people. Jonathan Teller-Elsberg et al report in the Field Guide to the U.S. Economy that "American Democracy is the best money can buy: in 2004, winners of seats in the House of Representatives spent 3.7 times as much as losers did". This inequality of campaign funding was also compounded by the fact that most winners were incumbents which already gave them an increased presence in the electorate. Here we have a classic case of positive feedback in action. The richer candidates are favored by the system which then provides them and their supporters the means to stay in power and increase their wealth, often at the cost to the poorer members of society. Simply put, the rich get richer and the poor get poorer, and the system encourages this. A survey in the Field Guide to the US Economy showed that between 1983 and 2003 the average income for households in the top 5% grew by $108,987. The gain over this same period for the bottom 20% was $9,996 which is $839 in real terms. This increase has been completely negated in many households by the inflation rate of the most essential item, housing. In some areas such as Los Angeles house prices doubled in the five year period from 2000 to 2005. What makes this drop in real income more unpalatable is that the workforce has generally become more efficient in this period, producing more product per man hour than ever before.

This inability of the poor to influence elections generates such cynicism and apathy that it is not surprising that only 45% of low income families turned out to vote in the 2004 presidential election. In total, 64% of eligible voters turned out compared with turnouts of 75% in Europe. Unfortunately there is no automatic connection between a candidate's ability to attract funding and his/her relevant knowledge base, management capabilities, or ability to contribute to government. The feedback loop is therefore severed and Gaian principles are contravened. There is of course a strong connection between the special interest contributors and the support for their case by the candidate when in power. Many members of Congress recognize that contributions from special interest groups should be curtailed and further patches will be applied to discourage the worst excesses. I do not believe, however, that this problem will truly be eliminated until sweeping changes are made to the way elections are funded, Congress is structured, and industry is taxed and subsidized. Not until we change some of these fundamental issues can we begin to revitalize democracy in the U.S.A.

So how can these fundamental issues be eliminated, or even reduced? Let us begin by considering the process to elect the President. The primaries cost candidates and their supporters many millions of dollars, and deter many competent potential candidates from putting their name forward. It would be possible to eliminate the whole process by allowing Members of both Houses of Congress to nominate the candidates for presidential elections. After all, the Members have all been voted by the people to represent their interest in Government. The objective would be the nomination of presidential candidates for Republican, Democrat and Independent parties. Funding for the final election by the people would best be provided by each party machine, and no direct funding to the candidates should be allowed. This would insulate the successful candidate from the sources of funding and no personal obligations would arise directly to such sources. (It goes without saying that the anachronism of the Electoral College should be eliminated as it is without merit in today's computerized society.) I hope this proposal will be given serious consideration and public debate, for the parliamentary method of nomination would have a number of advantages. The most important consideration is that the successful candidates will have the full support of their party in Congress and would most likely be nominated because of their leadership qualities. They will have already demonstrated leadership and managerial qualities and have no requirement to be exceptionally rich. Also, the Congressional Members will be incentivised to choose a presidential candidate who will likely be successful in addressing the pressing issues of the period, since their own futures in Congress would depend on that success. Members of Congress will also be more committed to support their own nominated leader in addressing the big issues of the day. This is a significant point which emerges mostly in difficult and important circumstances. For example, I believe that if Congress had supported President Woodrow Wilson in his proposals for dealing more leniently with the defeated Germans in the peace negotiations leading up to the Treaty of Versailles in 1919, the reparations demanded in the Treaty would not have been so harsh. Hitler would not then have found such fertile ground in the disgruntled population, and the Second World War would not have occurred. Similarly in 1993,

President Clinton was elected in a large part to fix the health care system in the U.S. In the event, the Democratic Congress which was expected to support a proposal for a more universal health care system, did not cooperate either among themselves or the Executive to develop an acceptable proposal. The result was chaos, with seemingly every second Member of the House coming up with their own proposal, and nothing was achieved. It is always on the big issues, where strong and sometimes brave leadership is required, that the system of checks and balances is counter productive. Consider the late President Gerald Ford's brave move to pardon former President Nixon. If the full power of the checks and balances had been brought to play, the country would have been in a sorry state for several years following Nixon's resignation. As a result of President Ford's brave decision, he relinquished his chance of a second term. Unfortunately the big issues of today are hardly debated between the executive and the legislative arms of government. Issues such as increasing income inequality, global warming, health care, education standards, strategic development of infrastructure, simplifying taxation, reducing drug use in society, improving the quality of life, and many more issues which need to be urgently addressed, have no forum for discussion between the two elements of government. Press conferences and prepared speeches by staffers are a poor substitute for open debate such as occurred in the exchanges between Gladstone and Disraeli in the 19th century British Parliament. The President of the United States is not called to account in open debate or cross examination, except during the process of impeachment. This has allowed presidents to break the law with impunity on a number of occasions. The most recent being the unlawful wire tapping of suspected terrorists which has been done without a judge's warrant.

The principal of no direct campaign funding should also be applied to all Congressional candidates. Independents could form their own special interest party to which contributions could be made. Funding should be obtained from the central party organization and allocated as seen fit by the Party. The only obligations which would then arise are the obligation to the Party, and the rightful obligations of candidates to their constituents. Prospective candidates who demonstrated their ability to attract funding for the Party would tend to be favored when it came to the choice of candidate, so there would still remain some lesser amount of connection to funding activities. However, such a system of party funding would be in danger of nominating only old party hacks who had little or no real world experience, so in addition to such a change, it would also be advisable to consider a change in the qualifications for eligibility of Senators, and Representatives.

Since 1787 the only qualifications imposed for Congressional candidates are that they should be of a minimum age, an American citizen for a minimum number of years and reside within their prospective constituency. Imposing term limits would be one way of keeping Congress fresh. Unfortunately, a Federal court rejected a proposal for term limits (often referred to as Initiative 573) in Washington State in 1994 on the grounds that it is unconstitutional. This decision came after similar measures had already been passed in 14 other States. The will of the people in this regard is definitely being thwarted. To change candidate qualifications will require a Constitutional amendment. This can be achieved by either a vote for the proposal by two thirds of the members of both Houses of Congress, or by three quarters of the State representatives at a duly called Constitutional Congress, or Amendment Convention, to consider Constitutional amendments, as allowed in Article 5 of the Constitution. We cannot realistically expect State Representatives to vote away their jobs nor, in recent years has there been a large enough majority of one party in Congress to vote for Constitutional changes. In fact all of the States at one time or another have applied for an Amendment Convention, so that today there are 567 such applications which have been ignored by Congress. The organization, Friends of the Article V Convention has instigated two lawsuits to try to force Congress to call an Amendment Convention but so far, without success. With such strong barriers against reform, there would appear to be no hope of any sweeping change until a groundswell of opinion becomes a tidal wave for change. New leaders will need to emerge to power the wave of opinion, imbued with leadership skills and energy to press for change both inside and outside Congress. Unfortunately, most Members of Congress have become a sort of unwitting cartel of lawyers. They have a common interest to maintain the status quo in exactly the same way as the aristocracy of Europe in the 18th and 19th centuries. For example, the vast majority of members of the Senate are white males whose only prior experience is in Law or Government. Oddly enough, female Representatives and female Senators are in exactly the same proportion of 16%. In 2008, only two of the 100 Senators, Chuck Hagel and Robert Bennett, list any prior experience in business which is sorely needed in today's economic turbulence. The one characteristic above all others which is needed in our politicians is leadership. Today, the man in the street is bewildered by the effects of the flattening world on his future prospects and should be able to look to political leaders for guidance. Unfortunately, our political leaders are totally unaffected by the process of outsourcing and off-shoring and are more likely to incite unrest than offer sound advice and leadership. There is a desperate need for more broadly qualified, entrepreneurial leaders to steer us through the stormy waters many are experiencing today. The Members of Congress may have been voted to represent the people, but they are certainly not representative OF the people, nor do they constitute a healthy diversity of experience. Bill Gates noted that "when you meet with Chinese politicians, they are all scientists and engineers. You can have a numeric discussion with them—you are never discussing 'give me a one liner to embarrass (my political rivals) with.' You are meeting with an intelligent bureaucracy,"

It is my contention that the cream of academic talent is attracted into Law because of the elevated and protected nature of the profession, and the ease with which they can make seven figure annual incomes. The practice of Law has become an increasingly inefficient monopoly of lawyers whose jobs are protected by both the Constitution, and their colleagues in Congress. Court cases which used to take a few hours now often take months to come to an unsatisfactory completion, and real justice is not served. Not only will attorneys never see their jobs outsourced to China, or face competition from global labor forces, their relative standard of living will continue to increase, by allowing the profession to become ever increasingly inefficient and their living costs pegged by cheap import of goods and labor. If Congress was stuffed with Farmers, does anyone doubt that food would be far more expensive? Congress needs a more diverse array of talent and it would be preferable that no one sector of the population should be allowed to dominate either House. Congress has talented, legally qualified staffers who draft the Bills passing through both Houses. There is no pressing reason therefore why nearly all Senators and a large proportion of Representatives should be qualified lawyers, particularly since most do not have any experience outside the machinations of the Law, and only a few have in depth experience in executive leadership of others.

The State boundaries of 1787 roughly grouped people of similar mind and occupation, farmers in Virginia; white Anglo-Saxon protestant industrialists in New England; Dutch and Swedish interests in New York and Pennsylvania—etc. A second House, the U.S. Senate, was instituted as an afterthought, to placate the Founding Fathers who were from the smallest of the 13 States. They would have been outnumbered in a system purely decided by voting districts based on population, so a compromise was worked out. Representatives were to be voted from districts of roughly equal population, and each State, irrespective of population, would return two Senators (originally chosen by State Legislatures). This two House system has worked well to ensure that serious consideration has been given to each new Bill which is passed into Law. Despite the demonstrated need for an Upper House of the Legislature, it cannot be claimed to be entirely democratic, and there is no evidence to show that it works better today than when the State Legislatures appointed the Senators. Milton Friedman's central teaching was that a free market economy must be based on choice, which is allowed by competition. He also pointed out that a free market economy could only exist in a freely elected democratic system. Today, California with a population of nearly 38 million people has more voters than all of the smallest 22 States combined, but still only elects 2 Senators. Some senators have as few as 300,000 constituents, while the California Senators represent over 16 million constituents each. This is on a par with the "rotten boroughs" of 18th and early 19th century England. It is high time that we should consider other systems which eliminate disenfranchisement of large sections of the population, and provide more choice of candidates, and a greater depth of experience in Congress.

I believe the State is no longer the best vehicle for defining the constituents of the Senate. With the help of today's technology, it would be very easy to group populations in many different ways, some of which may not be defined by physical districts These alternatives should be investigated and discussed before the present system becomes atrophied, and American society goes into decline. Presently, about 75% of US households have access to the internet, and this continues to increase yearly. The internet could become a means for electing candidates, and a vehicle for defining electoral groupings (districts) based on occupational affiliation as opposed to physical districts. If a central, secure data base were set up, as suggested in chapter 5, this could be employed to define every person's identity and affiliation, and allow them to vote electronically according to that affiliation. For example, each party could nominate candidates from each of the disciplines which contribute to the life and government of the country. There could be categories for legislators, civil servants, farmers, teachers, industrialists, health care workers, career military, factory workers etc. If the number of senators were allocated to each category roughly according to the population in the category it would provide a form of proportional representation. It would also ensure a voice for each sector of the population in the Senate, without the need for lobbying, while still maintaining a multi-party system. There are other ways by which the Upper House could be composed, which can be allowed by application of today's computer and internet technology. My fervent hope is that some alternatives will be explored, since this is one way that the great U.S. democracy could be refreshed for world leadership in the 21st century.

The process of government, the actual governing of the country, also would benefit from an in-depth study. It can be compared to parenting; good parents define boundaries for their children (laws and statutes at the Government level) and then ensure that no incursions across the boundaries are allowed. It is counter productive to set the rules and then not be assertive in the policing of them. I am sure that the country would benefit from a stronger, more assertive Government. One which sets the rules and then ensures that non political and non governmental institutions are empowered to manage the various needs of modern society within the boundaries of those rules. The Government needs to get out of the business of management of such functions as Medicare, the Registry of Motor Vehicles and many other institutions and functions which would be better managed by industry in a competitive environment. There are many examples of weak Government today, from the millions of illegal immigrants which are tolerated; critical infrastructures such as bridges and levies not maintained; emergency management forces unready for emergencies, to multiple DUI offenders who are allowed on our roads. It seems to me, that the U.S. government in all its various parts does not govern, but makes deals in order to get things done. Much is made of the checks and balances formulated in the Constitution between the Executive, the House of Representatives and the Judiciary. There are also checks and balances within the House itself which gives the impression of the trading floor of the Chicago Board of Trade rather than that of government. The "pork" added to even the most urgent of Bills passing through both Houses of Congress is nothing short of bribery and is a disgrace to the democratic process. The attitude of "you allow my earmark and I'll allow yours" has lead to the ridiculous position of 12,000 earmarks added to bills voted in 2007. Several attempts to patch the system have been made, the most notable being the allowance of a Presidential line item veto. Even so, pork barrel spending has become an epidemic, from a total of 8 earmarks per year during President Reagan's administration to the many thousands added today. I would contend that it is time to consider dismantling many of the systems of government, and take Thomas Jefferson's advice that every generation should write its own constitution. The elimination of all campaign contributions to individual candidates and all campaign funding totally from industry would be a start. In Lincoln's Gettysburg address, he defined his concept of democracy as "government of the people by the people". He said nothing about corporations or special interest groups governing the people nor did he envisage government of the people by rich lawyers.

In 1787, when drafting the Constitution, it was necessary to preserve sovereign rights of the individual States which had, for a number of years, previously existed as independent States. The United States was referred to in the plural until after the civil war when for the first time it was regarded as a single country. It is now high time that petty State jealousies are set aside to bring in a unified system of Law, taxation, education and social and environmental standards. This would have many practical benefits as well as the elimination of duplication of Government services. Only when we have a single set of statutes governing the Law can we begin to reclaim a fair system of justice. Philip Howard in his book, The Collapse of the Common Good asserts that Americans won't be free to do what's reasonable until judges take the responsibility of deciding who can sue for what. This principle will be impossible to re-establish within the jurisdiction of 50 differing State legislatures. For example, on January 14th 2007, an article appeared in the New York Times regarding Alabama Law. Jack Cline, who allegedly contracted leukemia from exposure to benzene at work in Birmingham, was not allowed to bring suit against his company under Alabama Law. His case was thrown out by the Alabama Supreme Court citing that there was never a valid time in which Mr. Cline could have brought a suit. Alabama law requires people exposed to dangerous chemicals to wait until a manifest injury develops. When his leukemia developed years later it was too late. Alabama's statute of limitations requires that suits be brought within two years of exposure. In just about every other State in the Union, Mr. Cline would have been allowed his day in court. I see no valid reason today why any separate State Law is required at all. Why cock fighting is allowed in two States for example when almost the entire World has banned the sport, I cannot imagine.

Elimination of State Laws in favor of a single set of Federal regulations will unfetter U.S. industry and allow it to compete more effectively in the Global marketplace by eliminating much of the bureaucracy associated with the differing State regulations and taxes. It should also allow for State income taxes to be collected by central government and distributed on an equitable basis. The levying of State sales tax has become almost impossible to enforce since an ever increasing number of purchases are made over the internet, many using eBay. Differing State taxation also causes the ridiculous situation where many people commute many miles to work in another State to take advantage of the difference, and in doing so consume a large proportion of the imported oil.

There is a need for smaller, stronger, and more responsible government, but several organizations and vested interests will argue that placing more power at the Federal level is making for BIG GOVERNMENT. I will show how a stronger Government can result in less bureaucracy, increased accountability, more responsibility and a reduction of personnel and cost. Of course, if you are a cockpit owner in Louisiana or a brothel owner in Nevada you would decry the Big Government in the same way as the slave owners of the South did in the second half of the 19th century. I have no illusions that it will be easy to bring about any of these changes, but the task will not be as challenging as that which the founding fathers faced in trying to free themselves from the yoke of British Colonialism. The same spirit of determination and enterprise which was shown by the Founding Fathers will be needed by the people today to reclaim democratic government from the vested interests now in control.

Chapter 5

Taxation

Taxation has been the subject of massive volumes in all the media around the world. Much has been reported about the complexity and injustice of the American taxation system, but I would note at the start of this chapter, that I believe it is more important to attend to how the tax is budgeted and spent than how it is collected. Too little time and effort is spent in devising more efficient systems of government and tax collection. Despite all the rhetoric to the contrary, you cannot reduce taxes without reducing spending, otherwise you are merely burdening future generations by our fecklessness. However, there is nothing that stirs up unrest and disaffection in any population more than an unjust system of taxation. Historically, when working people could not pay their taxes and leave enough for a subsistence living, revolutions and insurrections have followed. Implementation of an equitable system of taxation that is simple to operate will probably provide the most calming effect on any society. The effect may be even greater than any temporary reduction in taxes themselves. There is nothing new in this thinking, even the Joint Committee Report of the US Congress in April 1997 stated that virtually all economists agree with Joseph Stigliz, Chairman of President Clinton's Council of Economic Advisers that "Three main traits define a well designed tax system: fairness, economic efficiency and simplicity. Generally targeted tax policies do not meet any of these criteria."

In the past, our politicians have shown that they cannot be trusted to manage our hard earned money once it gets within their grasp. Nowhere is this more evident in their management of investment in Social Security retirement funds. The Social Security Trust Fund was set up separately from the general Budget funds to provide a funded pension for all the contributors. This has been a gigantic con. trick by our political leaders, for although today there is a healthy surplus in the current account, this has been raked off and used to pay for other government programs. Today, there is no money or investments in the Trust Fund, but a whole lot of IOU's from the government. This profligacy on the part of our government means that no growth in the Fund has been made such as should be expected in a 401K program for example. This is not the only Trust Fund run by the government which has collected money for specific purposes and then not used all the money collected for that purpose. Medicare and Aviation Trust Funds for example have been raided for use in the general Budget and are now in a very precarious state. It is my contention that government has shown itself to be incompetent to manage many of the areas of society for which it presently has responsibility. Government should get out of the business of managing healthcare systems, retirement plans and other functions which can be managed more efficiently by competitive market based operations. These functions should be funded by Government from taxes, but the management of the service should be competitively bid by industry. Not only do we need to look at the system of taxation, but how government spends the taxes collected in order to achieve the goals that are desired.

There is a great pressure for improvement of the taxation system in the U.S. which has prompted a number of politicians to advocate a change to supply side taxation. Unfortunately this does not either reduce the cost of government or improve the efficiency of collection or the surety of collecting the tax due. If the tax on income were replaced by a sales tax on all goods and services, excluding rent and mortgage payments, the level of Federal sales tax may reach as high as 40%, since the 2007 federal budget spend is 20.1% of GDP. This level of sales tax would inevitably lead to wide-scale tax evasion and smuggling, so I believe other solutions should be sought. Proposals for flat taxes on income are gaining support in several countries. Chile and Estonia for example have recently emerged from the grip of totalitarian government and have adopted flat tax systems in their new market economies with spectacular success. I am a great believer in flat taxation which is both simple to operate and easy to report by the taxpayer. Such systems will almost certainly spread throughout the world as more countries see the benefits brought about by flat taxation in neighboring countries. Unfortunately flat tax systems may unduly burden the low income earners unless they include substantial personal allowances, the elimination of which was one of the reasons for proposing the flat tax in the first place. Newt Gingrich proposed a flat tax system in his book "Real Change" that had a personal allowance, before the tax is applied of $13,200 together with a $4,000 exemption for each dependent child in addition to the current $1000 tax credit per child and the current earned income tax credit (EITC). Such a system may be easier for the tax payer to report, but it would not allow any economies to be made in government itself, and the same amount of tax would need to be levied as with the current system. My own proposal is that a flat tax should be levied after every adult citizen and green card holder residing in America has been provided with a subsistence income from the Federal Government. If this Federal Income is set at the proposed net minimum wage (after tax) for 2007 for a 40 hour week for example, each adult would receive a tax free Federal Income of $10,721 per year. Any income thereafter would be taxed at a flat rate with NO allowances. This proposal would go hand in hand with the abolition of all government welfare and disability programs, child tax credits, social security and payroll taxes. Whole government departments would be redundant and major cost savings would be allowed. The amount of taxpayer's money which would be retained and used in the Government's budget could be reduced by many billions of dollars, thus releasing more money into the market economy. The two tax rebates provided by the Bush administration may have worked to provide a stimulus to the economy, but it came at increased Government cost of collection and redistribution. The proposal for a flat tax coupled with a Federal subsistence wage distributed through nominated banks will reduce government costs, but even without the staffing and the collection efficiency improvements that will be made, the Government's budget could still be balanced by levying a flat tax of 35%, which is the same rate of tax that is presently levied at the top rate of income tax. I believe this represents the fairest system of taxation where everyone receives the same Federal Income and pays the same rate of tax. The very simplicity of the system in which all taxes are levied by employers, including domestic employers of part time workers, will more easily ensure compliance and will help recover the tax gap of unpaid taxes, which in 2001 was estimated by the IRS to be $290 Billion.

The total cost of the Federal Income which could be paid to every person over the age of 21 will be about $2.27 trillion. The flat tax will be much easier and cheaper to collect, and could be extended into other areas of taxation such as Corporate taxation and capital gains taxes. To those who would claim that we cannot afford such a burden on the taxation system, I would point out that the real amount of tax which is spent on Government overhead will be reduced substantially. Also, 25% of Federal taxes already go to social security programs and a further 17% goes to programs targeted towards low income families and the unemployed. A further large proportion of the Federal Tax goes to pay Civil Servants who collect tax and control welfare payments. I would estimate that a budget of about $3.7 Trillion dollars would be required to pay the Federal Income and pay for all the non social security and welfare programs currently in the Budget. The total income of everyone in the US, not including the existing welfare payouts is about $12 trillion. The flat tax level would probably be set at about 35% of everybody's income initially, but after efficiencies have been achieved and more people are gainfully employed, this could be reduced. The one allowance which I would envisage would be for investment into a self managed retirement fund at a maximum rate of 10% of income say. If all taxpayers contributed 10% from their income into such a fund, the effective tax rate would be reduced by 10% to 31.5% of income. This would gather $3.78 trillion, more than enough to balance the Budget. Incidentally, a taxpayer who invests 10% of income into equities in a Portfolio for Life for 40 years would, on average, accrue sufficient capital to take an income from the investment equal to final salary.

Under such a system, everyone in employment would contribute at the same rate to the cost of government and government programs. I suggest that such a fair system would engender greater commitment and reduce the divisive feeling that the present system has caused particularly among the working poor. Even Warren Buffett, the celebrated billionaire investment guru commented on the unfair system of taxation in an interview with NBC's Tom Brokaw in October 2007. He reported that he did an informal survey of federal taxes (income and payroll tax) paid by his own office staff and the average was 32.9% compared to his own rate of 17.7%. This means that presently, the people who can least afford it are paying a much greater proportion of their income than those who can easily afford to pay more.

One aspect of Milton Friedman's monetarist economic theory is the concept of a "natural rate of unemployment". In his famous Nobel Memorial lecture of Dec 13th 1976 he noted that "A highly static rigid economy" (e.g. communism) "may have a fixed place for everyone whereas a dynamic, highly progressive economy, which offers ever changing opportunities and fosters flexibility, may have a high natural rate of unemployment." This natural rate is only reduced by ACCELERATING inflation and increased by accelerating deflation. It seems strangely prophetic that the other famous Milton, the poet John Milton, noted in his sonnet "On His Blindness", "They also serve who only stand and waite". The unemployed are now recognized to be a natural part of life in a free market economy, so there is no reason why we should not support them and allow them to subsist without excessive hardship. The unemployed can then more easily retrain, and be more selective in the alternative employment opportunities they consider. This will increase the efficiency of the workforce which would be encouraged to rise to the highest level of competency. Underemployment of talent would be discouraged which would increase income levels and general prosperity.

The existing welfare programs do not encourage recipients to seek paid employment since when they do become employed, the support from welfare programs is stopped. Existing means tested welfare also acts to discourage two parent families to live together to bring up their children. Payment of a Federal income would be a positive incentive for couples to live together to share costs and raise their children. The present system of welfare is another example of positive feedback which encourages the opposite result from that which is sought. All such programs should be phased out, and to a much lesser extent replaced by Federal funding of admirable charities like the Salvation Army, Red Cross and the mentally handicapped charities, who can best look after the special cases, and the hardcore unemployables. There would be no need of a statutory minimum wage, since everyone would already be receiving Federal Income at this level. This would eliminate government intervention in both income regulation and welfare payments. The result would be fewer government personnel and further encouragement of a market driven economy. I predict that this would have the same rejuvenating effect on American society as the new market driven economic policies did in Estonia and Chile.

Distribution of the Federal Income would be most efficiently managed by the large banks with the help of modern personal identification technology to eliminate fraud. Such systems are already in use on a smaller scale in high security installations and in some German banks and supermarkets. This could be organized in conjunction with a national identity security system, which itself could be run together with a national drivers license. Everyone in America could be enrolled onto a national biometric identification system at their local Registry of Motor Vehicles, uniquely identifying everyone in America. The identity system would in turn be used by the banks for national identification purposes thus eliminating the need for credit card pins. Any two people whose biometric identities were determined by the central computing system to be close could be resolved by ordering the two people in question to report to their local banks at the same time, thus eliminating any attempt to collect more than one Federal income. The same biometric identification would be used by the banks, credit card companies and the Transportation Security Administration. The cost of setting up and maintaining the system could be totally offset by charges levied on banks and credit card companies who could use the universal security system for their own customer's transactions saving many millions of dollars by elimination of fraud. This has lots of positive consequences, only those enrolled on the system will be able to get Federal Income, driver's licenses and bank accounts. International terrorists would find it very difficult to penetrate the transportation security or remain in the country without being identified. It would also be possible to eliminate most of the TSA screeners at airports by allowing known passengers who have been previously vetted and biometrically identified to pass through security with minimum checking. Illegal immigration would be discouraged because immigrants would be more surely taxed than before with no offsetting Federal Income and they would find it impossible to obtain a drivers license, credit card or bank account in America. They would also compete with previously unemployable American citizens who would be drawn back into employment with low paid, but rewarding jobs. The cross-border economic pressures would therefore be reduced, resulting in fewer illegal immigrants.

Social security investment for pension purposes would best be made into a personal account in an approved bank or other investment house. Each adult would own his own portfolio of investments which I will call a Portfolio for Life (PFL) and will come back to this later. Government should set the rules for pension planning and provide regulatory oversight on investment companies, but should get out of the business of organizing and funding pension plans. The Federal Government would be already providing a catch-net baseline income before and after retirement, but the banks distributing the Federal Income would be tasked with the responsibility of ensuring that each person was contributing to a bona fide savings plan. If a bank client below retirement age could not offer proof of payments into such a plan then the bank would be empowered to withhold a part of the Federal Income in order to fund a basic retirement plan. There is a precedent for this today for example in mortgage lending. If the borrower cannot show proof of insurance, the bank or mortgage lender will buy the insurance and charge the borrower.

Payment of a Federal Income has many positive implications for today's social issues. The changing employment scene means that many redundant workers need to be retrained, these people would be able to exist for a period on their Federal income without the fear that this will stop before their retraining is complete. If a Federal Income is instituted, there will be no need for a minimum wage, therefore some of the jobs which are now being exported or performed by illegal immigrants could be available at lower rates to those who cannot find skilled employment. There is no doubt that America will be best served by a well educated and trained workforce, but flexibility and mobility in employment must be encouraged if we are to continue to make economic progress. The factors militating against flexibility in employment are (1) fear of being without an income; (2) fear of being without health insurance and (3) a lack of retraining facilities. Many people accept part time employment and under employment rather than risk being without an income. It has been estimated that in 2004 when the unemployment rate was 5.5%, the total underemployment rate was 9.7%.

One further important point to note is that if payments began at the age of 21 for example, students who would otherwise not consider going to college could delay their further education until they reach 21 when they may have amassed some savings, and could get the extra support needed from Federal Income. Another important aspect would be that convicted felons would assign their Federal income to help pay for their incarceration. Yet a further advantage would be in tracing and ensuring that deadbeat dads paid their child support. Their Federal Income could be directly attached by a simple court order, and they could not hide in the national identity system, since everybody would nominate a bank to receive their Federal Income. It would be unnecessary to find the dead beat, just his or her bank. No civil servants would be needed to operate the system which would both reduce the cost and frustration of dealing with demeaning government welfare systems.

The collection of the flat tax would be, as it is now, the responsibility of the employer. Today, if the employer is not registered, part time workers and low paid workers often escape being taxed. There is always the doubt that such workers are liable for tax because of the various personal and professional tax allowances. The flat tax system would remove all such doubt, since there would be no allowances to set against income and the very first dollar would be taxed at the flat rate. A report by the Government Accountability Office (GAO) estimated that the amount of tax payable to the Government which was unpaid in 2005 was between $312 and $359 billion. Under this proposed system of flat tax, every dollar earned would be subject to the flat rate of tax, and would be much easier to identify and collect. Only bona fide registered companies contracted to do work would not be eligible for the tax since they themselves would be the employers, and would collect tax from their own employees. Private individuals who employ a part time gardener for example would be required to pay the flat tax on any payment to their employee. Non payment could be discouraged by levying a penalty on the employer of twice the unpaid tax liability, for example. We can begin to see how we can regain control of both the tax collection process and illegal immigration. The level of inescapable income tax would be a major disincentive to illegal immigrant laborers, but the country may need to legally import foreign labor on a temporary basis. One way around this would be to institute a system of invited guest workers. A legally invited guest worker for example would not be eligible for Federal subsistence wage, but could have a special reduction in the flat tax rate. This would be a strong incentive to enter the country legally. Finally, no green card should be granted to anyone who could not show that he had employment which would generate more tax than the Federal Income paid out.

Under this proposed system which does not allow for tax offsets, payments to charities would be negatively effected. This could however be simply overcome by allowing charities to claim the flat tax back from the Federal Government at the flat rate paid by donors to the charity. This is a common practice in Europe.

Income tax is of course just one of the taxes levied on us today. Many investors make a good living without receiving any regular salary, and avoid income tax payment altogether. Their income may be derived from profit made in buying and selling equities which would attract capital gains tax. Capital gains taxation is a complex subject which needs better understanding. If, for example, an investor invests in a gold bar and sells it for more than he purchased it, has he made a real gain? If the currency were still tied to gold then no gain would have been made. Also, if he rebuys that same bar, he has simply reset the dollar starting value of his investment, but has the same asset value as before. He would however be required to pay the capital gains tax on the gain made when it was sold. If capital gains tax is levied on all such "paper" gains, we are in danger of the Government eating the seed corn of our capitalist society. On the other hand, especially during the 80's and 90's, many growing companies did not pay dividends on the profits they were making, but left the income in the company to provide increased share value for their investors. Long term capital gain, when realized, attracts a much lower rate of tax than the rate of income tax. Short term gain which is largely made by people playing the market can almost always be regarded as a "real" gain and ought to be taxed at the same flat rate as income. The problem comes in how to define and determine real gain in some calculation which may be index linked. The present system which taxes low income workers at 5% and others at 15% for long term gains does favor the people who derive their income from investment over salaried workers. Perhaps this is needed to encourage investment, but it is certainly divisive, and when the measure is passed by a Congress full of rich investors one can justifiably question the motive.

I would like to propose a new system of taxation which seeks to simplify as well as make capital gain taxation more equitable with earned income taxation. For this, I envisage that all taxpayers hold a Portfolio for Life in a federally regulated investment company or bank. Payments into the PFL up to an allowed proportion of income (10%, say) would be before tax which could be claimed back at the end of the year. This would be the only offsetting allowance in the flat tax system. Each individual would have complete control of his/her investments in the PFL. The type of restrictions placed on investments in 401K plans to invest only in mutual funds for example must be eliminated. Only in this way can real competition and choice be restored to the millions of employees who have seen their investment in their pension plan fail to achieve the gains made by even a conservative index such as the S&P 500. They have also seen their investment in Social Security make no gains whatsoever. I propose that any and all trades made inside the PFL should be free of all tax. Thus there would no longer be any concept for tax purposes of capital gain or capital loss. Only when payment is made out of the Portfolio for personal use should tax be levied at the flat rate of taxation. The purpose of the investment company holding the PFL would be to ensure that the regulations are complied with and to levy the flat rate income tax on all distributions from the PFL. Capital gain made outside the PFL could be taxed at the flat rate of income tax. The banks and investment companies holding PFLs would also prevent any PFL investment in items for personal use such as boats, aircraft, jewelry or works of art that should be purchased from taxed income. The investment company could also act as investment consultants, but should in no way restrict the choice of investments by each individual PFL holder. This system has the added advantage of eliminating the need to have a specific retirement date at which a pension can be taken. Income from dividends can be taken at any time and taxed at the flat rate at the source, but if they are paid back into the PFL, tax allowance or rebate could be claimed. After retirement, any income paid out of the PFL would be taxed at the flat rate of taxation, so the net effect of the movement of money into and out of the PFL would be simply to delay the tax liability in the same way as investment in a 401k plan operates today. It would however allow everyone in the country to participate in increased valuations in the global economy, and have a stake in the prosperity of the world at large.

Corporate taxation has generated much bitter comment from overburdened taxpayers who see companies spend small fortunes to avoid tax. According to a February 2004 report issued by the General Accounting Office, an estimated 61% of U.S. corporations paid no federal taxes between 1996 and 2000. The subject is a minefield of pitfalls for any authority attempting to collect corporate taxes. The State of California imposes a tax on corporate profits of 8% but finds this so difficult to collect that they impose an alternative minimum tax of $800. Over 80% of the companies operating in California pay only the $800 minimum tax. At the Federal level, US corporations operating globally have myriad opportunities to defer paying taxes. Foreign subsidiaries of U.S. companies are required to pay U.S. corporate taxes on their profits, but by a simple paperwork change, they can change the subsidiary into a "controlled foreign corporation" and defer all tax repatriation indefinitely. Congress itself provides U.S. companies loopholes, tax shelters, subsidies and preferential treatment. Indeed, the capitalist system makes it incumbent upon the captains of industry to safeguard their shareholders interest by paying the smallest amount of tax for which they are legally obliged. Also, many economists see companies as legal paper entities, not to be treated in any way like a person. They are the geese laying our golden eggs and as such should be exempt from tax. There is some recent economic evidence to support this view from the European Union. The country with the lowest rate of corporate taxation, Ireland, has shown remarkable economic gains relative to the other member states. The economy and employment opportunities are now so attractive that a reverse emigration from America to Ireland has begun.

Recently, changes in the rules governing taxation have allowed many companies to "check the box" and act as a pass through entity for taxation. This has been the system by which most small "S" corporations have been taxed for many years. I would go even further and allow all U.S. corporations to have a zero rate of corporate tax on profits. But coupled with this, every mature company should be regulated to pay out to its shareholders on an annual basis, a significant proportion of its profit. (I suggest that 50% would be as good a starting point as any other.) These dividends would be taxed at the flat rate at source. By this means, the tax would be levied on people who are company shareholders, and not the company itself. Since the flat rate will likely be somewhere in the vicinity of 35%, the effective income to the treasury would be 17.5% of all corporate profits. This is well below today's corporate tax rate of 35% but way above the rate which is actually collected after all the allowances and loopholes have been employed. Under such a scheme, it would make no difference where these profits were made, or distributed. Foreign shareholders of US corporations would pay the same flat tax as U.S. citizens. Other common methods of international tax free transfers such as foreign management charges could be taxed in the same way as income, at the flat tax rate. U.S. subsidiaries of foreign corporations would be treated in exactly the same way, forcing 50% of profit to be distributed back to the parent and taxed at the flat rate in the U.S. Also, any dividends distributed to US citizens from foreign corporations in countries without tax offset agreements, would be taxed at the flat rate. Thus there would no longer be any advantage for American business's to be headquartered off shore.

There would be other advantages of forcing dividend payouts, which may be reflected in the stock markets. The original intention of all stock markets was to allow easy access for industry to find finance. Today, it has become much more of a gigantic gambling casino, where bets can be placed on whether stock prices will go up or down, with no regard to long term investment in any particular company. Many brokers and hedge funds make money by shorting stocks in a process in which the fund effectively borrows stock which it does not own, and sells it short, only buying it back when the price has been forced down by their selling activity. This has contributed to much of the extreme short term market volatility which has been a characteristic of most western markets since the mid nineties. One factor which will inhibit short selling is the need to pay any dividend which becomes due to the owners of the stock which has been borrowed. The dividend will be paid out to the new owners of the stock, which could represent a substantial loss to the short seller. If dividends are paid out quarterly, then short selling will only be done over short periods, and market volatility would be reduced.

I am a great believer in the fiscal discipline engendered by the need to pay dividends. It imposes monetarist principles on the board rooms of U.S. companies. Indeed some of the worst excesses of the corporate world would be eliminated by this requirement. I am convinced that if all companies had been forced to pay a dividend, it would have resulted in greater fiscal controls over the cash in the business. In some companies such as Enron, it would have revealed that the declared profits were more like the proverbial emperor's new clothes. The story of Digital Equipment Corporation (DEC), which never, during the 40 years of its existence, paid a dividend, was that the shareholders would best benefit from reinvestment of the profit back into the business. This state of affairs continued until the company went into decline and started selling assets in 1992 to stay alive. Finally, it sold the remnants of its computer operations to Compaq in 1998, without ever paying its shareholders a penny, other than from the final fire sale.

The case against payment of a high percentage of profit in dividends has been the perceived need to reinvest the profit to achieve greater growth. In very young companies, it may be necessary to reinvest all profit since more working capital is usually needed for increased inventory and receivables in a growing business. But for all mature companies, I would like to debunk this concept. Organic growth is produced by successful new product and market development, but all R&D and marketing costs are already applied to income before tax. If necessary, all operating income could still be reinvested in R&D, but under existing accounting policies, this would erode the declared profit. Far more frequently, accumulated income has been used to acquire other companies which frequently do not result in greater income per share, so that existing shareholders do not benefit from the acquisition. Acquisitions however, do invariably result in the formation of larger companies in which the directors and senior executives pay themselves much greater income, bonuses and stock options. If the Board of directors had to seek further funding from the shareholders for prospective acquisitions, justifications would need to be made and this would have the same effect as monetarist policies on national economies. The choice would be given to the shareholders whether to invest or decline and a good case for the proposal would need to be made to the shareholders by the Board, thus encouraging a greater openness in the company.

In summary, I would like to point out the simplicity of the proposed taxation system where there is only one type of tax and one flat taxation rate. Only people or foreign entities would be liable for tax, and companies would not spend large amounts of senior executive's time in devising tax avoidance strategies. There would be less motivation to move large US companies off shore, and perhaps some would return to the fold. Tax revenue from companies would increase, and armies of accountants who are currently occupied in tax mitigation could be redeployed in more productive activities. Internal government spending would be reduced and several million civil servants would be released into profitable employment.

Chapter 6

The Law

In chapter 4 a recommendation was made to abolish all State laws and legal due process in favor of a single unified system of Federal Law. This could not happen overnight, but assuming enough pressure were brought to bear from a concerned public, consideration of such a proposal could begin by a conference of State Judiciaries. Probably the first item on the Agenda of the Conference would be the method by which Judges are appointed. This is so varied from State to State, that it would become immediately obvious that the proposal is long overdue for consideration. The various methods of appointment cannot all be right, or even good. For example, the practice of public election of Judges is clearly open to corruption, and the public is largely not competent to determine any particular candidate's suitability or qualification for office. When judges are elected publicly, election funds need to be raised which opens the process to even more abuse than in the election of Members of Congress. Trial lawyers ensure that their protected position is maintained by contributing to the election campaigns of political and judicial candidates who support the status quo. It is a status quo in which personal freedom to do the right thing has been replaced by fear of stepping on others "rights". In my view, an essential first step in the recovery of real freedom is to establish a judiciary who cannot be second guessed by judges in some other court. Then all judges could be encouraged to take responsibility for making value judgments particularly in deciding who can sue for what. These value judgments would eventually become precedents in the same way as all other common law precedents. A hierarchical system with one unified method of appointment should be adopted for the whole of the U.S. New appointments could be decided by the existing district or circuit judges themselves, but since they have already abrogated their responsibility to exercise value judgments in court, they may find this a novel concept. One way would be for new judges to be appointed by their peers in much the same way as partners are elected in today's Law Firms. Such appointments are always made after the senior partners have gained some evidence of the new candidate's credentials and abilities. New appointments to the Supreme Court could still be made by the President and confirmed by Congress, but I would suggest that appointments are made from a list of suitable candidates proposed by Supreme Court members and senior judges.

Once we have a unified system of Law throughout the U.S. then we can begin to address the issues which are so well identified in Philip Howard's book "The Collapse of the Common Good". The worst aspects of today's litigious society have resulted from the trumping of authority by individual rights and the subsequent refusal to accept personal accountability. This needs to be urgently redressed if we are to save our schools, health services, and even our democracy from further decline. Successive governments have shirked their responsibilities to govern the people by not empowering those in authority in our schools, hospitals and local government, and have instead pushed this responsibility into the courts. In the courts, the judges have in turn pushed the responsibility onto juries. Control of the population by legal dictates has replaced human judgment and common sense in many areas of our lives. An attitude pervades that all issues between individual members of society and between members and those in authority should be decided in a court of law. The pursuit of "legal entitlement" has replaced any consideration of doing the right thing.

I believe that some of the worst excesses can be relieved by some simple procedural changes. Firstly, all speculative litigation would be prevented by automatic payment of a successful defendant's legal costs and court costs by the losing plaintiff. Presently these are only paid when the suit is deemed to be frivolous, but then a whole new hearing needs to take place to determine whether the suit was frivolous. As a result, the payment of defense costs by losing plaintiffs is as rare as rocking horse dung. I once acted as expert witness for a group of engineers in a start-up company in Florida who were defending themselves against charges of theft of trade secrets from their previous employer. The defendants won on all counts, but went bankrupt shortly afterwards under the burden of their legal costs, which is the result that the plaintiff sought to achieve. When a trial lawyer takes on a plaintiff's case on a contingency basis, then he/she should also share the legal costs of an opposing successful defendant on a "joint and several" basis with the client. To ensure prompt payment, a bond to the value of "reasonable costs" could be placed with the court before trial. This would ensure that the hearing would be as brief as possible in order to keep costs down, and efficiency of court use would be improved. Such assumption of responsibility would be a remarkable departure from the present system where attorneys do not guarantee their work, even for simple conveyance jobs. One has to take out title insurance, usually sold by the attorney involved, to have any chance of recovering from the negligence of that attorney. Can this be allowed to continue in the same country which espouses billion dollar medical malpractice payments, money-back-guarantees, the lemon law and the 100,000 mile guarantee? Of course it can while ever lawyers are running the country.

If the practice of paying a successful defendant's fees were implemented, then there would be far fewer cases taken to court. Some of the prospective plaintiffs would not go to court because of the lack of necessary funds for deposit. This leads to my second suggestion that anyone who is injured on the roads, in work or hospital should get relief by automatic payment for injuries received on a national scale of physical injury compensation. This would be paid by the employer, the hospital, or the insurance company involved. All similar losses should be valued identically for legal purposes. For example if a concert pianist lost a finger in a road accident, he should not be able to claim any greater compensation than would a manual worker. It would be the responsibility of every person to insure any or all of his/her person to some higher level if needed. This is the agreed practice for compensation of victims of international airline accidents formulated by the Warsaw Convention of 1929 and subsequently modified in The Hague Protocol of 1955 and The Guatemala City Protocol, 1971. These protocols limit the liability, except in cases of gross negligence on the part of the air carrier, to about $100,000 for each person killed in an air disaster. This is the liability of the air carrier irrespective of fault. In 1975, an International Conference on Air Law, convened under the auspices of the International Civil Aviation Organization (ICAO) adopted new amendments to the Warsaw Convention as amended by the Hague Protocol. Under these new provisions, the carrier is also responsible for cargo damage, irrespective of fault. To the devotees of litigation, this is an anathema. They would claim that absent the threat of litigation, there would be no incentive for the air carriers to protect their passengers and certainly no incentive to improve the safety record. How wrong they are, for the record of airline safety is nothing short of exemplary and is being improved by a planned 25% annually. Contrast the record of 428 air passenger deaths out of 4.2 billion passengers world wide in 2004 with the death rate in U.S. hospitals from causes unrelated to the patient's original condition. A study by HealthGrades released in August 2004, reported that an average of 195,000 patients died due to potentially preventable, in-hospital medical errors in each of the years, 2000, 2001 and 2002. Dr Samantha Collier, HealthGrades' vice president commented that this was "the equivalent of 390 jumbo jets full of people dying each year to likely preventable medical errors, making this one of the leading killers in the U.S." What is even more eye opening is that more medical malpractice suits are heard in court than any other type of suit in American society. According to the Bureau of Justice Statistics, between 1996 and 2001 the median awards made for medical malpractice were sixteen times greater than in all other tort trials. As malpractice premiums increased rapidly between 1996 and 2001, the number of malpractice awards remained stable, but total dollar awards increased from $371 million in '96 to $596 million in 2001.

Clearly litigation has not worked in American society to improve safety and security. The myth that litigation is necessary to make industries and others in responsible positions toe the line is a falsehood perpetuated by the legal profession. Today, it would appear that the threat of litigation is forcing good doctors and schoolteachers out of their professions and they are being replaced by practitioners of lower capability and dedication. Personal responsibility exercised within efficiently operated, competing organizations is much more likely to provide improved safety and quality of service than is the threat of litigation. The ability to exercise free choice in a competitive market will ensure that the forces of a free market economy will come to bear. Free market forces invariably encourage a process of continuous improvement. Litigation is getting in the way of that process and should not be allowed to clutter our courts except in cases of extreme or criminal negligence. Willful or criminal negligence could be identified by a judge during written pre trial proceedings which could be conducted before any case is heard in court. The proposed system would not preclude victims from being compensated, but windfall awards would not be made. There is no good reason why non criminal cases cannot be tried in specially appointed courts without a jury, such as is the practice for bankruptcy, maritime and family disputes. Sentences, awards and other punishments should be left to the decisions of Judges who are themselves periodically updated with recommended sentencing rules. Such a change could be tempered with a requirement for automatic compensation by hospitals and all employers for death and injury in service or during hospitalization. Compensation payment would be made irrespective of fault, and would be promptly paid thus avoiding much hardship on the part of bereaved and distraught families. No further compensation would be available to the victim, even if the defendant in the case were found to be guilty of willful negligence in a subsequent trial. The defendant would be subject to punishment by the court, but fines would be paid to the court, not to the plaintiff. In this way, the taxing of our hospitals, doctors, pharmaceutical companies and other industries by the legal profession could begin to be curtailed, and the cost and quality of healthcare will inevitably improve.

The practice of payment of punitive damages is one which has been devised by lawyers for the benefit of lawyers. In no other country in the world is this practice allowed. Courts in Europe for example have refused to grant punitive damages that have been awarded in U.S. courts. In 1985, fifteen year old Kurt Parrott was thrown from his motor cycle in Opelika, Alabama. He died when his helmet buckle broke and his head hit the pavement. Kurt's mother sued the Italian helmet manufacturer and was awarded $1 million in punitive damages. The company refused to pay and his mother pursued the case in the Italian courts, but the Italian Supreme Court refused to uphold the decision. The Court commented that private lawsuits brought by injured people should only have one goal which is compensation for loss.

I have shown that the practice of punitive damage awards does nothing to reduce the probability of future injury to members of the public by providing a deterrent. On the contrary, there are several instances related in Chapter 1 where the threat of litigation has exactly the opposite effect. An organization under threat from suit will inevitably cloak its operations in secrecy so that improvement of practices becomes impossible. Also, it is only PEOPLE who commit crimes, companies per se cannot be guilty of any crime, and punitive damages levied on companies must be eliminated. There is no such crime as collective negligence, some person or persons are always responsible for errors, emissions or crimes. Guilty persons should be sought out, and prosecuted to the full extent of the Law, and should not be protected by the corporate shield which may otherwise pay for their criminal fine. If a person dies because of a surgeon neglecting to scrub his hands properly, then the surgeon could be prosecuted for negligence and also the member of management who may have been responsible for defining and ensuring proper hygiene was maintained. The fact that litigation is likely to increase further business for lawyers rather than reduce further harm to the public seems to escape everyone. It would be much better for all concerned that punishment for negligence (not criminal negligence) should be policed by the hospital authorities and the Medical Society who can better ensure that standards (e.g. hygiene) are set and continuous improvements made. It is often the case that the threat of litigation to an organization will cause members of the organization to close ranks, and the true cause of the problem is never revealed and hence not eliminated in the future. The prompt payment of a standard compensation sum made to the victim's family should be just one incentive to ensure improvements are sought. All companies and institutions such as schools and hospitals should be free to remove any member of staff for poor performance, willful negligence, or criminal activity, thereby restoring the rule of authority within the organization. We cannot expect improvements to be made in any organization which does not have control of its members.

One way to encourage more responsibility and accountability on the part of all lawyers in the U.S. would be to form a Law Society to which all attorneys who want to practice law must belong. Presently, there are a number of U.S. Bar Associations National, State and Local, to which attorneys may voluntarily belong. These are not regulatory bodies which police their members, but are more like clubs where members can chat about issues. If you visit The American Bar Association's web site you will find listed the benefits of belonging to the Bar Association; —discounts at rental car companies, deals on computers, favorable loans—etc. The public needs more protection from unscrupulous attorneys without getting government forces involved. Why should F. Lee Bailey get away with lying in a court of law in which a murder case is being tried while Martha Stewart was sent to jail for a much lesser lie while attempting to cover for a friend? If it were compulsory to belong to a Law Society headed by Supreme Court judges, then this could have teeth to ensure all attorneys were properly qualified and in compliance with the rules of conduct. They could disbar attorneys for criminal acts, negligence and some misdemeanors which may not find their way into court. An annual fee could be charged to members that could be used to keep the membership updated on legislative issues and to provide malpractice insurance. Any wronged client would not need to litigate against his/her attorney, which is extremely difficult, but would apply to the Law Society for redress. Such a system would place responsibility where it rightfully belongs and where any professional misdemeanor can be detected and corrected. For example, if an attorney is negligent in title searches and the client subsequently has a problem with the title, the Law

Society would pay any and all costs to make the client whole. It would then be up to the Law Society to investigate the attorney and decide if he/she should be disbarred for being negligent. The Law Society would be motivated to keep the good name of the profession and to keep down the cost of legal malpractice insurance by disbarring frequent offenders. This principle of control by an Industry Association will be considered for other professions and industries and could lead to less government intervention in many areas of life today.

Chapter 7

Control of Industry and Financial Institutions

The U.S. is one of the few countries in the world which allows punitive damage awards in court. In chapter 6, I made a case for abolishing punitive damages against corporations and other institutions on the grounds that they did not succeed in forcing improvement, and taxed the public with higher costs. Legal costs and litigation awards made in 2006 against the pharmaceutical industry in the U.S. exceeded the total cost of manufacture of their products. There is no wonder that prescription drugs cost more in America than in any other country. Alex Azar, general council for the U.S. Dept. of Health and Human Services (later, deputy sec. DHHS) estimated that defensive medicine prescribed solely for protection against litigation raises healthcare costs by between $70 and $126 billion a year. Most of us would agree that many corporations and institutions have in the past made serious errors and allowed the goal of short term profit to override other considerations. So how can industry improve its record without resort to litigation? For some of the answers we can look for example at the product safety of the best companies. The top tier quality companies have adopted a policy of continuous product and process improvement within a rigorous quality system as defined by the International Standards Organisation (ISO). Most people will recognize this standard since many companies have declared their award of ISO 9000 in banners across the access to the company. It has been a milestone in many companies for which they should be duly proud. The standard has now been adopted by about 900,000 companies in 161 countries, and has replaced many of the military standards and inspection processes by military organizations throughout the world. In very simple terms, the standard forces a strict routine of

Say what you do.
Do what you say.
Record when you have done it.

There are only a few universally applied rules, and most companies define their own processes and acceptance standards. For example, in building wooden houses it may be sufficient to apply general tolerances of 2mm say, but in building aero engines, tolerances of one micron may be required on occasions, and are defined by the manufacturer. Much effort is put into getting it right first time, as opposed to earlier systems which relied on routine inspection of the product after manufacture. Companies such as GE Aero Engines, strive to reach and maintain the level of perfection known as "six sigma". This is a statistical measure based on the standard deviation usually identified by the Greek letter sigma. For those outside the field wishing to have an introduction to this standard of quality control I would recommend they read a short book "What is Six Sigma" by Pete Pande and Larry Holpp. The companies operating at six sigma level, manufacture the product or service to specification 99.9997% of the time. This can, and does happen without being compelled by regulatory requirements or threat of litigation. Market forces define what level of quality should be produced. For example, if Rolls Royce engines were demonstrably more reliable than GE engines, then they would win most of the market. Poor quality in the air is apparent to everyone when a disaster is caused by faulty equipment. We need to get the same transparency in other walks of life, but hopefully we can do this without great disasters.

Many aspects of our daily lives happen without any regulatory involvement by government. The government does not determine which type or size of potato we can buy in stores, although the government in Europe would. Some parts of industry are however still regulated and controlled by government workers. The FDA and USDA vigorously guard the quality of our food supply literally with a stamp of approval. We should now move on from this and allow the market to define the quality required. The producers in turn would define their quality procedures and set improvement goals. I guarantee that standards will surely improve when this is implemented. The marketplace is much more sophisticated than it was when the FDA was founded in the early 19th century when adulteration and misbranding of foods was commonplace. Today, large supermarket chains will vigorously relay the demands of their end customers to the producers. If all farmers and food processors were required to become ISO certified, then the ISO quality engineers from prodigious companies like Lloyds of London or Underwriters Laboratories(UL) would provide the inspectors to firstly ensure that each farmer and processor had a quality assurance system which met industry standards and regulations. On the subsequent annual visits, they would check for compliance and progress in the process of continual improvement. When the farming community signs up to this method of quality assurance, the instances of bacteria on salad crops will surely diminish. The FDA and USDA would continue to set regulatory requirements which would become part of each producer's quality procedures. For example the recent rulemaking by the FDA to eliminate specified risk materials (SRM's) from animal feeds to prevent the spread of bovine spongiform encephalopathy (mad cow disease). The cost of becoming ISO certified for a small farmer is not excessively burdensome, but could be offset by government grants since government's own costs would be reduced. It would also allow each farmer to compete by offering their own quality stamp to replace the USDA stamp, and could offer different crops and methods of production such as organically farmed foods or crops grown without pesticides etc. Consumers would soon learn to look for the quality stamp of their favored and trusted suppliers. Small farmers could group together in order to gain better recognition in much the same way as the Appellation Controlee system operates in the wine industry of France. The only regulatory process in which government inspectors may become involved is to join with the ISO to examine the credentials and performance of the Registered Inspection Companies.

    This same principle of ISO control could be applied to other industries which would release thousands of government workers and inspectors back into industry where they can better serve the country. Consider the pharmaceutical industry which is regulated tighter than a jailhouse, yet still new drugs are allowed on the market that are subsequently found to be dangerous. This happens despite the long and tedious testing and trials conducted by the FDA. There is an argument which asserts that since the FDA biochemists have vetted a drug, the government has deemed it safe and therefore to some extent releases the pharmaceutical company from product liability when things go wrong. (Indeed, some Government Agencies such as the Transportation Security Agency do provide a protective umbrella to their equipment suppliers to protect them from suit in the event of a terrorist attack.) Unfortunately, the FDA scientists do not have access to the pharmaceutical company's internal records to see what concerns they may have had during the development and trial processes. The pressure on research and field trial technicians from a management under its own pressure to meet the quarterly numbers often stifles internal comment in the hope that the concern will not be a problem in the marketplace. This process must be changed, firstly by allowing the Law to target guilty people within an organization and secondly giving the responsibility to the pharmaceutical companies themselves to perform the tests and trials within a strict formal quality regimen that would be regulated by the FDA. Failure to implement a quality system which meets all regulatory requirements would be grounds for shutting down the company. The Board's fear of being shut down will be greater than any fear of litigation to their company. But fear is not enough; all non executive boards must be required to have among their members a technically qualified person or persons who can act as watchdog on the quality assurance system and product liability issues in the company in addition to the legal and financial expertise normally found on company boards. This board member should be present at the annual Quality Review and receive all the reports from the ISO 9000 inspection company. It would be up to each pharmaceutical company to determine what resources to apply to the trials which could then be completed as fast as resources and regulations allow.

Control of quality by the ISO 9000 process could be extended into most of the corporate world including preparation of accounts where it would be advantageous to see a signature of the responsible person on each of the subsidiary accounts which are consolidated at the corporate level. Traceability would be much improved beyond the Sarbanes-Oxley compliance rules instituted after the recent rash of corporate crime. Banks and other financial institutions should be compelled by legislation to define their own in-house policies and procedures in a formal Quality Plan. Proper training and retraining in the quality procedures would become an essential job qualification. Each stage of any financial transaction would be checked and signed off by the person performing the procedure. For example the procedure for considering a mortgage application would have a checklist of questions and calculations, the answers to which could only be obtained by an employee or contractor to the bank, who would sign confirmation that all checks had been performed. Banks would be free to set many of the acceptance standards, for example, the maximum credit that can be extended to an applicant as a factor of income or the maximum that can be loaned as a factor of the asset value of the item to be mortgaged. The Government could enforce quality standards in Banks by guaranteeing deposits only in the Banks that are in compliance of the relevant ISO standard.

The reliance on credit ratings supplied by credit agencies should be discontinued, since often the rating system serves only to identify the profligate members of society whom the credit companies will find easy prey. The major contributing factor to the credit score is the payment record of the borrower. However, the borrower can make minimum payments by taking out more loans on another credit card. This process can increase the credit score of the borrower, since the more credit that is granted to the borrower, the higher will be the credit score. Furthermore, if the borrower only makes minimum payments, his/her credit score will be higher than a person who pays off all debt each month. So the increased debt allows access to yet more credit. This positive feedback situation can continue for quite some time until it finally collapses in the disaster of bankruptcy and more toxic debt infecting the banking system. Other ways of assessing creditworthiness must be investigated at the same time as the privacy and security of personal financial data is improved. In chapter 5 I recommended that each person should nominate a bank through which the federal income could be distributed. This bank could also hold the details of the client's income as shown on the last tax return. The bank could also be required to keep the total of all debt taken out by the client, and no loan could be granted without notifying the borrower's nominated bank. Thus the bank would have a record of all income and debt for each client, but this information should only be accessible on the presentation of the client's own biometric identification. Only the institutions which were authorized by the client would receive the sensitive personal data for the purpose of making financial decisions, but this data should not be allowed to be stored in any place other than the client's bank where it can be protected with a biometric key.

Another Wall Street problem that has recently become much worse is the volatility of stock prices. The original purpose of all stock exchanges was to provide companies ready access to financing. The concept of investment in well managed companies with good future prospects has been hijacked by the gamblers now in control of many of Wall Street's operations. My own opinion is that we should allow gambling on horse racing and other sporting events in the high street where the gamblers can only affect their own future, and eliminate gambling on company stocks which can adversely affect millions of people's livelihood. Allowing gambling on the stock exchange by shorting stocks or allowing derivative trades shatters the confidence of real long term investors. It also produces a Wellsian situation where the richer investor can prey on the lowlier investor, since the latter are not allowed to participate in hedge funds or short stocks. Investment for pension purposes and 401K plans has become a lottery, even when the companies themselves are performing well. It is an accepted premise in capitalist economies that speculators operate to provide a ready market, so that when one wants to purchase a stock it is available for purchase. This is the system of all shopkeepers. Dealers nominated by a company should be allowed to freely buy and sell the stock of that company, but all others who want to invest in the stock should be required to hold it for at least six months say. This would eliminate short selling and much of the volatility of the stock markets and return the confidence of the long term investor. It sometimes appears that market nerves and volatility is encouraged by those who make their living in Wall Street. Unfortunately, institutions have been set up to take advantage of the present system and the resistance to such a change by the seven figure players on the Street will be enormous.

The disciplines imposed by the ISO 9000 quality procedures can improve almost all organizations, but it may be difficult to implement ISO 9000 quality assurance procedures in places such as hospitals where many key people are not staff members. Many hospitals go through a process of accreditation conducted by the Joint Commission on Accreditation of Healthcare Organizations (JCAHO). The accreditation process is in many ways similar to the ISO certification process. Unfortunately, accreditation has not produced the improvements which must be made to reduce the number of deaths in hospitals caused by reasons other than the original ailment. Adoption of ISO quality processes would mean that consultants and contractors working in the hospital will be integrated into the Quality Plan which submits them to the disciplines and training of the quality system. Most hospitals have already instituted quality and security systems, but these can be improved by rigorous metrics which provides the feedback necessary to set up a formal process of continuous improvement as required by the ISO quality procedures. It may be a shock to the system to be expected to make problems visible as opposed to covering them up as at present for fear of litigation. This legal fear is preventing real improvement in our hospitals today. Contrast the present stagnant safety situation with the more open situations in some of the best industrial companies. Toyota, for example, has engineered its rise to the number one spot in world automobile markets by "mutual ownership of problems". In Toyota, employees are encouraged to report problems which are then tackled by teams of technicians and engineers to overcome the problem. Once the threat of litigation is removed from hospitals they can begin to instigate continuous improvement policies which must embrace all staff, consultants and contractors. Nobody should then be allowed into the operations of the hospital who has not received the training necessary for the position. The fear of litigation must be removed by eliminating all malpractice awards and replace them with an immediate, automatic payment to a standard schedule of compensation without recourse to court. For example, loss of life due to causes not connected with the patient's initial symptoms would be compensated by a hospital at the same fixed sum across the country for a person of that age. People who enjoy a very high income such as professional sportsmen or movie stars may claim that their earnings expectations are much higher and deserve a higher compensation. In such cases, the patient should insure their own lives and limbs to some higher value. Loss of other body parts and functions would all be valued at some lower level for the purpose of compensation and published nationally. Malpractice suits should be allowed for criminal offences only, but the victim should not receive any more compensation than that already paid at the standard rate. When it becomes apparent that a system based on these recommendations provides greater safety and security, I am sure patients admitted to hospital will vastly prefer to forgo their previous "right" to sue for large sums of money in place of being admitted into a much safer environment where patient's treatments are decided on best medical practices rather than what is legally expedient.

The standard of care in doctor's clinics or health centers varies from clinic to clinic and across the country. The frustration level of many primary care physicians over the need to practice defensive medicine and the ever increasing cost of malpractice insurance is forcing many general practitioners and gynecologists to move to other fields of medicine. As a result the standard of healthcare is too low and too expensive. If you have the misfortune of contracting a disease with multiple symptoms such as Lyme disease, you may get bounced from one specialist to another for many weeks or even months before a correct diagnosis is made. Sometimes, by then the disease is chronic and cannot be cured. It has become incumbent on people to manage their own healthcare since it is by no means certain that one's primary care physician can or will take the responsibility. Unfortunately, healthcare as practiced by the hard pressed general practitioners in the US is not conducive to the process of continuous improvement. Each small practice is so busy tending the sick, and completing insurance company paperwork, that there is little time left for updating skills and information, or improving diagnostic techniques. This is where I believe the American Medical Association (AMA) can be of greater help. The argument for compulsory membership is the same as that which I made in chapter 6 for giving the American Law Society greater responsibility and authority. Physicians and surgeons should only be allowed to practice medicine after being accepted into the AMA. The AMA should be provided with the authority to police its own members and strike off those who fail to maintain an acceptable standard of care. Presently, the AMA offers voluntary malpractice insurance to its members. This should be extended and made compulsory so that it is recognized by all to be the body responsible for the standard of medicine throughout America. The AMA would be tasked to pay compensation promptly to patients who had suffered real problems as a result of the treatment or lack of treatment provided by one of its members. The AMA could also be tasked with ensuring that each doctor's office becomes certified to a relevant ISO quality management standard. JCAHO already acts as the accreditation body for hospitals and other healthcare organizations and would be an excellent candidate for an ISO certification company. Doctor Paul M. Schyve, senior Vice President of JCAHO commented that in hospitals, Accreditation and ISO 9000 can fit together and compliment each other. My own suggestion would be to have the accreditation process integrated into a new ISO standard so that more companies can compete to perform the inspections. In this way, the dependent relationship between the JCAHO and its clients would be eliminated. Also the increased responsibility to institute a program of continuous improvement should ensure progress in the effort to improve our healthcare services.

The role of government in the proposal to institute ISO 9000 quality planning throughout industry, agriculture and healthcare, although diminished in scope and personnel involved, is strengthened by setting improvement goals and regulations which will be assimilated into the procedures of each industry regulated. State and local government itself could be made more efficient by adopting the ISO 9000 quality system in their own operations. This can lead to improved controls such as those applied to sex and DUI offenders in the community. Government can also improve compliance in many areas by setting national standards. Standardization would be improved if Government departments were only allowed to buy from ISO 9000 certified manufacturers and suppliers. Government should also set engineering standards by purchasing only to those standards. It is ludicrous that Americans and American manufacturers are still clinging to the old British system of measurement by inches and feet, pints and gallons, pounds and ounces, BTU's etc. when the whole world has changed to the much easier and more efficient metric system. Government departments and public schools should in future deal only in the metric system. The rest of America would then be dragged kicking and screaming into the 21st century.

I cannot leave this chapter on the Corporate World without a comment on subsidies, and other common practices of protection of certain industries. There may be good national security reasons for protecting certain sectors of industry, or even of individual companies. We need a thriving defense industry in order to ensure that we are not at the mercy of an unfriendly supplier in a national emergency. We may also encourage U.S. industries to ensure that dependence on foreign supply of strategic materials is reduced. However, I would urge that all proposals for subsidies should be published together with a legitimate reason for such subsidies before they are made. All such reasons should continue to be published in advance of any increase in subsidies or protection together with a time limit of the protection. The principle of the greenhouse is demonstrated every spring, when many seedlings are given the protection of a hothouse during infancy but are then planted in the open where they continue to thrive without further protection from the elements. Young companies and industries should be treated like hot house plants, and offered some help to get off the ground. Mostly this help is obtained from financial backers, but government can and does play a part by financing the development of strategically interesting technologies and projects. The subsidizing of a mature industries such as the oil or farming industries can have no valid reason when all other mature industries have to adapt to the flattening of the world or go out of business. The long term application of subsidies leads to inefficiencies and higher costs, to say nothing of the burden on taxpayers. Rather than protect US Agriculture and other industries from foreign competition by applying subsidies, it would be much better to re-establish the free market conditions of healthy monetarist policies to provide automatic control of imports and exports. The reason why monetarist economics fail to balance imports and exports today is that the supply and demand for dollars and foreign currency is complicated by the reinvestment of dollars by foreign suppliers to the U.S. and the use of the dollar in non-U.S. trade by third parties. One simple monetarist way to balance imports and exports is to have U.S. Customs issue export vouchers to the full value of exported goods and services. These vouchers could be traded on a mercantile exchange for import permits. No imports would be allowed without a balancing permit which would have an expiry date of one or two years say. The system could be started by issuing export vouchers to the exporters of goods in the previous year. Also, in order to account for the trade which does not receive an export voucher, the import permit could be at some higher level of value than the actual export by a small amount such as 5%. The free market for import permits would ensure that during the time of a trade surplus, they would be worth very little, but at the moment, with an imbalance approaching a trillion dollars, those export tokens would be worth a considerable amount. The income generated from the sale of import permits would go directly to the exporters of goods from America, thus encouraging exports and discouraging imports until the supply and demand balance. Once this system of import control is in place, there will be no need to subsidize large oil companies to encourage domestic exploration, since this would be encouraged by the strong price differential favoring the home produced oil. This proposal could be implemented within a few weeks of passing the enabling legislation.

One further advantage of import permits will be obviated when economic stimulus packages are introduced to revive the economy. Some of the tax rebates granted in the past to stimulate the economy have gone directly to purchase imported goods which does not help the domestic economy at all. Making more money available to consumers will only revive the domestic economy when exports and imports are in balance.

Thomas Friedman explained in his book "The World Is Flat" that the forces of globalization are producing great changes to society and industry alike. Competition in the global marketplace is making many jobs fungible. I contend that the minimum wage is also acting to force these jobs offshore and making a sector of the population permanently unemployed. The obvious solution for the chronically unemployed and underemployed is to re-educate or re-train themselves for a different career. We must accept however that some of these people will not be able to achieve a higher level of training, or that other jobs may not become available. We should not assign these unfortunate people to the junkyard of permanent unemployment. For this reason, in addition to the Federal wage recommended in chapter 5, I would propose to abolish the statutory minimum wage, and allow the labor market to find the right level of wage. I do not envisage a massive return of the labor intensive industries to the U.S. as a result of the elimination of minimum wage, but at least sufficient low paid jobs may become available to provide rewarding employment to those who want it. The imposition of a minimum wage has been yet another example of positive feedback. It has been unnoticed by the legislators mainly because in the U.S. the effects have been masked by a huge influx of illegal immigrants who are outside the law and some may not be paid minimum wage. The higher the minimum wage has become, the greater is the pressure to move jobs off shore.

Monetarist principles and policies only work in free markets where there is a plethora of supply and demand. The labor market is no exception and will find the right level to balance the forces of supply and demand. There is however at least one glaring exception at the top of the market for certain CEO salaries. Many chief executives have bamboozled their Boards into making obscene awards in the form of salary, bonuses, stock options and severance payments. Boards have also offered favorable contracts to CEO's which are not generally available to executives and other managers at lower levels. My own view of the reasons for this is that at all levels below the CEO, any manager or employee can be replaced at reasonably short notice without fear of collapse of the organization. In other words nobody is indispensable. Management understands this and the labor market operates competitively. Unfortunately, some Boards live in fear of the CEO leaving because no Board member could take over the job even for a short period. This is where the laws of supply and demand break down since there is insufficient competition. I hesitate to suggest that government should legislate to stop the nonsense of sky high CEO remuneration, but some restrictions must be considered. Firstly, no stock options should be allowed to be granted below their price on the date of offering. (This has now been largely implemented) Bonus plans should be based on pre agreed performance values. Stock price, profit, sales or growth in sales could be used in some previously determined calculation to determine the performance related bonus. This should be required by SEC rules and published by each company in the annual report. Finally, no special pension or conditions of employment should be allowed that are not also offered to the other managers in the business. Each company should be required to publish a unified policy of severance payment which should apply to all employees including the CEO. New legislation will be needed to bring about a change to the present unsatisfactory position where failed chief executives have walked away with over one hundred million dollars compensation after being fired from the job. This practice foments unrest in the work force and is very divisive in the community at large.

Readers will no doubt by now have detected a common theme in all the proposals for more efficient regulation in a new capitalist economy. I propose that government should set the minimum regulatory requirements, but each industry and company will define their own procedures and acceptance standards in a rigorous quality system. These quality systems are designed to get the product or process right first and every time. The watchdogs on the quality systems are not government employees, but independent ISO inspection companies authorized by the government and the International Standards Organization. The cost to the taxpayer of the armies of government employees will be reduced to a mere fraction of the present cost. What is more important the proposals will allow the forces of free market competition to provide increased quality, reliability and safety. Improvement in quality of products, food supplies and financial services will be made immediately on implementation, and the process of continuous improvement will ensure that we will continue to enjoy improvements year on year. These measures can inject new energy in industry, the financial world and government operations and can restore the U.S. to world leadership in these areas.

Chapter 8

Reduction of Environmental Impact

Ever since humans first appeared on Earth, the species has had a disproportionate impact on local and global environments. The burning of forests to gain access to food in the form of dead animals probably began a few million years ago. Unfortunately, forest burning is still prevalent today, particularly in Brazil and Indonesia where forests are burned to clear the trees for ranching and agriculture and temporarily improve the fertility of the soil. In 2006, climate change also added a further effect, for the rainy season in S.E. Asia which normally starts in October, did not occur until November. The man made fires continued to burn out of control until November, by which time the whole area from Malaysia to the Philippines was cloaked in a thick haze. The situation in the Brazilian Amazon was even more frightening, the drought was so bad, that the mighty Amazon was reduced to a fraction of its normal flow. The forest became even more flammable and man made fires seen from satellite monitors, raged out of control. The United Nations Environmental Program (UNEP) published a global budget of CO_2 emissions in The Global Environmental Outlook 2000 which estimated that the total CO_2 emissions in 1999 from the burning of Savannahs, tropical and temperate forests, agricultural waste and fuelwood, amounted to some 3940 million tonnes annually. Compare this to the annual CO_2 emissions from burning fossil fuels of an additional 6518 million tonnes and you will begin to appreciate the enormity of the problem which Gaia faces in trying to keep the planet in a fit state for life. The biggest irony in this burning of forests and savannahs is that much of it is done to make way for crops which are no longer grown on their traditional grounds because these have been taken up with crops used for the so called bio-fuels. This is perhaps the biggest and potentially the most disastrous positive feedback catastrophe of all time.

There are two separate but equally important aspects to burning forests, the most obvious is the amount of CO_2 prematurely released into the atmosphere which most scientists now believe is contributing to global warming. The second is that the very trees which have been destroyed were the source of some of earth's oxygen supply, and a sink for CO_2. The burned trees had a capacity to remove CO_2 at many times the rate of the crops which replaced them. It never ceases to amaze me that a majestic mature tree may contain tons of solid material, nearly all of which has been supplied from the gaseous atmosphere. The wood however is only a temporary sink for the carbon which will over many years find its way back into the atmosphere in the form of CO_2 and methane as the wood rots or is digested by termites and other insects. One permanent sink for carbon is in the form of chalk and limestone deposits such as can be seen in the cliffs of Dover in England. These deposits are the shells and skeletons of aquatic creatures which gathered the calcium carbonate from a food chain starting with phytoplankton. Phytoplankton are microscopic forms of algae which harvest the suns rays in a similar way to the leaves on the trees, absorbing CO_2, and liberating oxygen into the atmosphere. Algae of all types are responsible for over three quarters of the oxygen generated and CO_2 removed from the atmosphere. There has been much written about the carbon cycle, and I will not add to those volumes, but for anyone interested in understanding this complex subject, I would recommend Jim Lovelock's book, Gaia, A New Look At Life On Earth, and his second book, The Ages of Gaia. In 2006. Jim published his latest book, the Revenge of Gaia which deals more specifically with global warming and the CO_2 greenhouse effect. Here, I will assume the contribution of CO_2 to global warming to be real and suggest ways to mitigate some of the worst offences in this gargantuan crisis.

The first step is really a no-brainer; we must stop all further deliberate burning of forests and savannahs by man. This is an issue far more worthy of going to war over than ever was the case in Iraq. If the governments of the offending countries cannot stop this rape of the planet, then severe sanctions should be applied. Satellite monitoring is now a routine process so the offenders can be readily detected. The problem is here and now, and we should not rely on volunteer charities such as Greenpeace, admirable though they may be, to do the work of government. The corollary to this is that all growing of bio-fuels must also stop immediately, since this is one of the worst positive feedback errors that people and governments have made in recent years. It is causing the cost of staple foods to increase rapidly and will inevitably result in unrest and civil disobedience in many poor nations.

The second step is to reduce the net level of CO_2 emission from the burning of fossil fuels to a level comparable to that which existed before 1970 when global temperatures first stared to show a marked increase. This is well below the target agreed in the Kyoto protocol which called for reductions of 5.2% below the 1990 level of greenhouse gas emissions. I would recommend that CO_2 removal from the atmosphere is achieved in a similar way to water clean up in sewage systems. Many water authorities in the US and the western hemisphere manage both the supply of potable water and clean-up and disposal of the waste water. The water companies typically base their charges on the quantity of water consumed. In Europe where the density of population compels waste water disposal in town sewage plants, it is much more expensive to process the waste water than to provide the potable water supply. The cost of potable water is about 80% of the cost of disposal of the waste water. It is immediately obvious if or when sewage is not disposed efficiently, the local environment becomes intolerable and unhealthy from the stinking pollution. Unfortunately low levels of CO_2 pollution are not detected or otherwise observed by human beings, but to life on the planet, the situation may be disastrous.

We can envisage a system in which the CO_2 produced by burning fossil fuel is removed in a CO_2 sequestration plant. Fortunately, CO_2 need not necessarily be extracted at the source, although it may be more efficient to remove CO_2 in the smoke stacks of power plants and gas flaring points where the concentration of CO_2 is the highest. The CO_2 produced by vehicles will be more easily removed from the atmosphere at some other point on Earth, since mixing in the atmosphere is very rapid. I would propose that all supplies of fossil fuel should be purchased with a certificate of equivalent atmospheric CO_2 removal, which incidentally has a mass roughly three times the mass of the fuel. Oil and gas companies could either set up CO_2 extraction plant or purchase the equivalent extraction service from other companies. Government would only play a regulatory roll in preventing fraudulent activity in this process. A whole new industry would grow up that may address the problem in new innovative chemical or biochemical methods. There may even develop a market for carbonate material which may be produced in vast quantities. It would be pointless to legislate for reductions and mandatory limits, as legislation of this type has never worked in the past. After the Arab oil embargo in 1973, an attempt was made to reduce the amount of gasoline used by vehicles. The automotive industry was regulated to produce a certain proportion of more fuel efficient models. The average fuel efficiency of cars and light trucks on the road in 1987 was 26.2 miles per gallon, but in 2004 the average efficiency had fallen to 24.6m.p.g. This is yet another case of government trying to force a result by legislation which has not worked to produce the desired result. The Climate Action Report published by the Bush Administration in March 2007, estimated that CO_2 emissions will grow nearly as fast through the next decade as they did the previous decade. Several bills have been introduced on Capitol Hill in an attempt to curb emissions since the success of Al Gore's documentary, "An Inconvenient Truth". Also five Western Governors have announced plans to cap and then trade carbon dioxide emissions. I do not believe that quotas will work to reduce emissions, especially since the proposals also include the possibility of trading quotas. This will result in the whole world maximizing the output of CO_2 rather than reducing it. Consider a situation where Americans wish to purchase pollution quotas from India where its citizen's consumption of fossil fuels is many times below the allowed level. Funds would flow from America to purchase quotas to allow greater CO_2 emissions in the US. These funds would inevitably increase living standards in India where increased vehicle ownership and fuel consumption would follow. The net result would be an accelerated CO_2 pollution in both countries rather than a reduction. A similar situation arose when neutron activation equipment was first introduced to monitor the sulfur content of coal used in power plant. The sulfur concentration is regulated to reduce the formation of acid rain. At the time, the high sulfur coal sources were not used because they exceeded the regulated level. However, as soon as on line monitoring became available, cheap, high sulfur coal was added to the low sulfur supplies previously used and the on line sulfur monitor ensured that the sulfur content was maintained just below the regulated level. Unfortunately this caused increased sulfur emissions above the historical emission from coal fired plant.

Sequestration of CO_2 from the atmosphere paid for by a charge on the fossil fuel is much more likely to yield the required goal of reducing the level of CO_2 in the atmosphere. If the US had taxed gasoline at the same level as in Europe, then the demand would have fallen rather than increased as it has continued to do over the past 20 years, and alternatives would have been more vigorously sought. CO_2 sequestration should begin immediately in the power plants and oilfield operations of the western nations and oil producers who have had the advantage of cheap fuel and have polluted the planet the longest. It is unrealistic to ask developing nations to begin such a program when the consumption of fossil fuel and subsequent emission of CO_2 is far greater in the U.S. than anywhere else other than the Arab nations around the Gulf. The oil producers of the Gulf flare off much of the petroleum gases, and manufacture potable water in energy hungry desalination plants. The per capita CO_2 emission in the U.S. is twice as high as it is in Europe and twenty times higher than India for example. It will eliminate international arguments about quotas or per capita reduction goals if the oil producers and coal miners pay for the CO_2 removal and charge the CO_2 extraction fee on coal and crude oil itself. Klaus Lackner, the Ewing-Worzel Professor of Geophysics and researcher at the Earth Institute at Columbia University has pioneered the technology to extract CO_2 from the atmosphere and inject it into alkaline mineral deposits underground for permanent sequestration. In an article posted 04/24/07 in the Earth Institute News Archive heralding "The First Successful Demonstration of Carbon Dioxide Air Capture Technology by Columbia University Scientist and Private Company", Lackner noted that "This is the first step toward making carbon capture and sequestration a viable technology. I have long believed that science and industry have the technological capability to design systems that will capture greenhouse gases and allow us to transition to energies of the future in the long term." The private company working with professor Lackner, Global Research Technologies LLC, estimated that a small extraction device measuring 10m x 10m could extract 1000 tons of CO_2 per year. On this scale, one million devices would be required to remove one billion tons of carbon dioxide per year from the atmosphere. Previously, Professor Lackner has estimated that the cost to sequester CO_2 would require a charge equivalent to 25 cents per gallon of gasoline. In today's volatile market, that is less than many service stations have increased the price of gasoline in a period of one week. The Earth Institute News article also pointed out that the capture device can be located at the point of sequestration, eliminating the current need to match CO_2 sources with sinks. For example the CO_2 originating from all those vehicles in Bangkok can be captured in an oil field in Alberta, Canada where it can be used for enhanced oil recovery.

It is supremely urgent that we begin the process of CO_2 emission reduction without delay. Sustainable energy sources must be dragged out of the laboratories and put into service right away, even if these do not look economic today. Only by putting them in service will we gain the efficiencies of mass production and find their true value. Hopefully some will emerge as winners. When I first tried to persuade the Federal Aviation

Administration to use explosives trace detectors in airport security, the detectors would not detect every explosive known to man, and the FAA was looking for perfection. In such circumstances, perfection is always the enemy of the good. We continued to do more research until the fateful day of September 11th 2001, after which, we could not deploy the detection systems fast enough. The alternative sources of energy which may be considered all have some drawbacks, but with a sensible portfolio of energy sources, we can get through the periods when the sun doesn't shine, or the wind doesn't blow or the waves do not roll in. The one source of clean energy which can be tapped immediately is nuclear power. This is already economic and environmentally clean. We do however need strong government leadership to eliminate the nonsense of storing depleted fuel rods on the site of the power station when there is much better and safer storage available underground. Nuclear power can also be used to electrolytically produce hydrogen from water. No technological breakthroughs are required to put hydrogen powered vehicles on the road today, and these would have zero pollution impact on the atmosphere. The main message on this topic is that we CAN stop the rise of atmospheric CO_2 level; we MUST stop the rise in atmospheric CO_2 and we must begin immediately to deploy systems for sequestering CO_2 at the same time as moving away from fossil fuel power sources. CO_2 emission or concentration goals should not be legislated since legislation of this type has never been shown to work. Rather we must get agreement on the international stage to pay for CO_2 sequestration with the cost of oil and coal. This is the only legislation that is required and international agreement should be sought without delay.

CO_2 pollution is the greatest but not the only global environmental problem caused by modern society. In the mid 1970's, routine measurements of the concentration of ozone in the lower part of the stratosphere showed that the ozone was being eroded at an alarming rate. The ozone in the lower stratosphere absorbs ultra violet radiation which would otherwise produce a hostile environment at ground level. The reduction of the ozone layer was caused by comparatively small amounts of chlorofluorocarbons (CFC's) emitted at ground level. These fairly inert substances used in refrigeration and some cleaning agents, found their way into the upper atmosphere where they dissociated under the intense bombardment of UV radiation forming free chloride radicals. The chloride radicals in turn acted as catalysts in a reaction to change ozone (O_3) into oxygen (O_2). One chloride fee radical could change many ozone molecules back to oxygen. So potent was this process in the Polar Regions that large holes have appeared in the ozone layer.

This layer of rarefied ozone gas acts to reduce the transmission of ultra violet radiation to levels which are acceptable to life at the Earth's surface. When an ozone layer hole appeared over southern Chile, the UV radiation was so intense it caused rabbits in the area to go blind. The international community came together and made a landmark agreement to phase out all CFC's in the Montreal Protocol of 1989. Kofi Annan described the agreement as "perhaps the most successful International Agreement to date". A timetable was agreed to gradually phase out production of CFC's, and meanwhile new refrigerants were produced which do not have such a serious effect on the ozone layer as the CFC's. Hydrochlorofluorocarbons (HCFC's) were made to replace the CFC's, but they have not been given a complete bill of health and will in turn be phased out by 2030 in favor of hydrofluorocarbons (HFC's). Unfortunately, the HFC's are powerful greenhouse gases and will need to be controlled if we are to avoid overheating the Earth even further. It is now estimated that the ozone layer will recover by about 2040. The CO_2 reduction will however take much longer to produce a turn round on the temperature chart even if CO_2 emissions are reduced today.

Pollution produced by industry, vehicles, and in our homes must be reduced for local as well as global reasons. Historically, severe local pollution was caused because it was cheap to dump industrial, domestic and agricultural waste in the local environment and rivers. Industry in the 19th century was guilty of fouling many rivers and lakes and of killing many delicately balanced ecosystems. Fortunately, in the Western hemisphere, this practice has been reversed, and for example, salmon are returning to rivers which were previously too polluted or dammed. Gains have been made by a hodge podge of regulations and good will of local communities. I would propose to go a step further and regulate that all factory effluents are treated at source and all products are sold with a prepaid and defined method of disposal. This would ensure that wherever possible, goods and packing materials would be recycled in the same way as empty cans and beer bottles are recycled with the help of a small charge added at point of sale. In England during the late 1990's the roadsides became littered with old vehicles which had reached the end of their useful life. It had become expensive to dispose of them to a wrecker's yard and so they were stripped of identification and left on the roadside. The practice has now been largely stopped by the imposition of heavy fines, but it would be much easier if the automobile industry had provided disposal facilities from charges made in the original sale.

Disposal of some products have a much more serious potential for causing pollution and even terrorist threats. Products which contain a radioactive source for example should be sold with a bond which would ensure their proper disposal at the end of their lifetime. Dr Henry Kelly president of the Federation of American Scientists in a presentation before the Senate Committee on Foreign Relations on March 6th 2002 reported that the DOE Off-Site Source Recovery Project (OSRP) had recovered and disposed of over 3000 radioactive sources used in universities and medical facilities. He commented; "Unfortunately inadequate funding of the program serves as a serious impediment to further source recovery efforts." Neither industry nor individuals should expect government or local government to fund the disposal of their trash or unused items. However, government should legislate for the infrastructure to deal with such disposal. We are already having difficulty finding places to dump the non biodegradable garbage, and our shorelines are increasingly littered with trash. To alleviate this, I would recommend a monetarist approach to the problem. If we had to pay a premium at point of sale to dispose of the non degradable items, particularly packing materials, then the use of non degradable plastic packing materials would very quickly be reduced.

The international community can and will work together to tackle some of the major global environmental issues, but we do need politicians with the integrity, will, and knowledge to address the problems during their tenure in office. Unfortunately, any pollution mitigation will lead to higher costs and reduction in material living standards. Pollution mitigation will therefore be politically inexpedient, but set against this will be the prospect of a healthier planet and improved chance that future generations may continue to enjoy life on this Earth. At the moment, we seem to be pushing all the major issues both economic and environmental onto the shoulders of our children and grandchildren. The baby boomers of today inherited a world in which their prosperity and freedoms were won by the heavy sacrifices of their parent's generation. It is high time that we in turn give up some of our creature comforts to ensure that our own children and their children's children inherit a world as beautiful and fertile as the one we are privileged to know and love.

Chapter 9

Facing the Threat of International Terrorism

In previous chapters, I gave an outsiders view on alternate ways to approach some of society's issues. I cannot claim to have intimate knowledge of many of the issues on which I have felt compelled to comment, but I hope I have been able to provide a fresh approach to looking at them. On the other hand, I do have considerable personal knowledge and experience of international terrorism. For the past 40 years I have designed and produced products for detecting and eliminating improvised explosive devices many of which are in use in our airports today. I have personally met with anti terrorist forces around the world; I have also trained explosive ordinance disposal officers and many security operatives. Our equipment has been deployed to protect many Heads of State and community leaders from the Dalai Lama to Oprah Winfry. The most important lesson I have learned during this time is that if you believe and act like you are involved in a "war" against terrorism, then without a doubt, you will lose that war. Terrorist organizations can be compared to the Lernaean Hydra which Hercules was tasked to kill. If one hostile head was cut off then it grew back another two. If foreign military personnel kill terrorists on their own soil, then it serves to stimulate others to join the terrorist organization. If that same occupying force kills innocent civilians, recruitment into the terrorist organization will soar. I think it would be better to approach the present Islamic fundamentalist terror like the medical industry has approached finding cures for cancer. This has been on many levels with many painstaking hours of trials and experimentation. There is no golden bullet, in fact, if we treat terrorism in our own minds as if it were a social cancer, then we can be on our way to containing the problem. There are still only a few cures for cancer, yet many cancers can be contained so that the patient can live a near normal life. One direct analogy would be to the treatments which reduce the blood flow to the tumor and keep the cancer in check. If support to the terrorist organization is cut off then the organization will die. Support in this case would be financial, moral, and ideological. While ever there is a large sector of the population that supports the terrorist goals, then confronting the terrorist organization with force will fail. Only in totalitarian regimes could this policy solve any of the problems. That is usually because totalitarian regimes have resorted to mass extermination and sometimes genocide to overcome the problem. This is of course intolerable to any democratic society, and we must seek alternate ways to deal with the problem.

We can learn much from the way the Western Nations dealt with the communist threat after the Second World War. The threat from the communist block was successfully contained for over 50 years. The only failure occurred in Vietnam when America supported successive regimes to militarily confront the regime of Ho Chi Minh who enjoyed considerable support in both the North and the South. The policy of containment as opposed to armed conflict requires great patience, and is politically unrewarding especially if you have dominant armed forces which are very tempting to use. Fortunately, throughout the period of confrontation of the forces of Communism, our political leaders largely kept their nerve and both sides held their armed forces in check. In truth, there never was any danger to the Western Democracies from communist ideology after 1945, since it had already been shown to be an economic system which did not work in any developed nation. The threat was from a well armed totalitarian regime which probably recognized that the longer the stand-off lasted, the more likely their political system would be exposed as the failure it indeed was. This was perhaps the greatest danger, and the whole world was lucky that Gorbachev became leader of the Soviet block at the very critical time when communism was finally exposed as a bankrupt ideology. If the Russian Generals had succeeded in their coup attempt in August 1991, it would almost certainly have lead to war with the West.

Extreme Muslim Fundamentalism is an ideology which has attracted many followers, and we must try to understand why this is before the movement can be contained. In 2001 at the time of the attack on the World Trade Center, Afghanistan was one of the centers of fundamentalism which was supported by the Taliban regime. Many of the Taliban leaders had been schooled in Madrassas, the Islamic religious schools some of which were sited over the border in Pakistan. These schools were financed from Saudi Arabia in the late seventies to provide anti Soviet forces with fanatical recruits to fight the communists. The schools were used to brainwash young boys in the teachings of Muhammad bin Abd al Wahhab, an early eighteenth century Muslim Fundamentalist, and to teach military terror techniques. The schools have become known in the West as Wahhabi madrassas and were featured in a PBS Frontline program after the Embassy bombings in 1998. Haroun Fazul, a native of the Comoros Islands off East Africa was believed to have conspired with two Saudi nationals to blow up the US Embassies. His training in the Saudi financed madrassa in the Comoros and subsequently in a madrassa in Pakistan was documented on Frontline in 1999 and subsequently in 2002. The technique of taking young boys and turning them into efficient killers is unfortunately not new. The British were very successful at teaching young boys killer instincts as midshipmen in the navy in the 18th and 19th centuries. Also, the Hitler Youth Organization which recruited boys as young as 10 years old was a training ground for many who subsequently joined the ranks of the SS where they became a fanatical fighting force. Saudi support for the madrassas which preach intolerance of all other religious groups, including more rationalist Muslims, may surprise many in the West. The breeding ground for much of the violent Fundamentalist teaching is in Saudi Arabia where 15 of the 9/11 hijackers were born.

I believe the reason for the support of fundamentalism by the ruling Saudi family is largely because they use Wahhabi teaching to legitimize their own rule and policies. This goes back to the early part of the twentieth century when Abdul Aziz ibn Saud began his conquest of the Arabian Peninsular, which resulted in the foundation of the Saud dynasty in Saudi Arabia. Saud gained early success in Najd in north-central Arabia, and determined to change the nomadic lifestyle of the people. He forced the formation of communities known as hijrahs around desert oases to cultivate the land and encourage the Bedouin and other nomads to settle down. Most importantly, he imposed a regime of Islamic fundamentalism by building mosques and staffing them with the Ikhwan, a religious para-military group who followed the teachings of Muhammad bin Abd al Wahhab, a past Sheik of Najd and supporter of the strict literal observance of the Qur'an. The Ikhwan became politically very important and in 1918 were recruited into Saud's army where they proceeded to conquer the districts of Hejaz and Asir which later were assimilated into the Kingdom of Saudi Arabia. By 1926 however, the Ikhwan began to have major disagreements with Saud over modernization of the country such as the use of automobiles and telephones. The rift widened by 1929 and resulted in several atrocities and murders which further escalated the disagreement to the point of civil war. The Ikhwan suffered a defeat at the edge of the Nafud desert after which the organization broke into two factions, and the leaders of the revolt were imprisoned. The Ikhwan who remained loyal were later absorbed into the Saudi Arabian National Guard, where they still wield some influence. Also, most of the religious text books in the schools of Saudi Arabia are still based on the ultra conservative teachings of Sheik Wahhab.

There is therefore a history of using fundamentalists to prop up the Saudi regime and to provide a focus away from the feudal policies of the Saudi Government. This is a real life case of "Wag the Dog" in which the ruling family of Saudi Arabia are using the fundamentalist bogies of Israel and the Great Satan (USA) to divert attention from the frustrations and brutalities of their feudal regime. This is a regime whose members may enjoy the luxuries and entertainments of Las Vegas but would rather let a group of Saudi girls die in a blazing fire rather than let them be seen without their Islamic covering. Unfortunately, regimes such as in Saudi Arabia, Kuwait, Sudan and formerly Afghanistan are now causing many Muslims to look to fundamentalism as an escape from their frustration at being impotent to make progress and instead are looking several centuries backwards. A religion such as Islam in which the Church has no hierarchical structure, must keep to the letter of the holy book to maintain unity of the faith. The vacuum created by the lack of leadership has been filled by politically ambitious groups and individuals who have used their influence for political rather than religious purposes. This has now been compounded by the thousands of brainwashed young men who are prepared to die and believe they will go straight to paradise if they can kill many infidels.

So how do we begin to make some changes you may ask? As I wrote before, there are no golden bullets, and it is my belief that no progress will be made while ever foreign troops are present in predominantly Muslim countries; Israel needs to get serious about solving the Palestinian homeland issue; and rational Muslims and the Imams must speak out against the heresies of fundamentalism, particularly the sins of suicide and murder. We could begin to influence these possibilities by political pressures, embargos and stopping subsidies to countries which do not cooperate. If Israel does not make progress in forming a contiguous, viable Palestinian Homeland, then the West should withdraw economic support from the Israeli Government. In the Muslim world, sponsorship of extremist sects must stop, and most importantly, the radical mandrassas must be closed down, or placed under the control of rational Muslim authorities. Anyone who has not seen the film,

Charlie Wilson's War will be well rewarded by seeing it. At the end of the movie, when the Soviets had been defeated in Afghanistan, the Zen Master's prediction of wait and see was left ominously unanswered. The CIA strongly recommended that money should be supplied to build schools to educate the 60% of children in the Pakistani tribal area abutting Afghanistan who had no schools. Unfortunately the failure to fund schools meant that the only schooling that many young boys received was in the radical Madrassas. This fuelled fundamentalism in Afghanistan and lead to the domination of the Taliban and the harboring of Al Qaeda. There is still an opportunity to change this situation by funding schools which will give young people self confidence, hope and ambition to look forward rather than backward.

These measures will not immediately stop Islamic fundamental terrorism, since the movement has gained tremendous momentum by the political and strategic mistakes made since the 9/11 attack on the World Trade Center. We played right into the hands of Al Qaeda by taking the war into Iraq which was governed by a regime hostile to Islamic Fundamentalism and to Bin Laden in particular. The leaders of Al Qaeda must not have believed their good fortune. The war eliminated one enemy and brought their greatest enemy within range and in conditions which made it very favorable for their operations and expansion of their membership. We must now be very patient, for progress will inevitably be slow until the more rational members of society throughout the Middle East and Asia can reduce the support for the extremist elements. Meanwhile, we must take passive defensive measures to contain the threat. America must reduce spending on military overkill to defend against some superpower emerging in the next ten years, and start to get serious about defending the population at large against terrorist propaganda and attacks on American soil. We should begin this campaign by issuing a national driver's license with biometric identity which could be used for security and financial transactions. The biometric could be two tiered with fingerprint and iris scans, for example, stored on a driver's license. For low security applications, only one of the biometrics would be required, but for applications where the person must be uniquely identified, both may be required. All banking and financial transactions should be allowed only after biometric identification using one or both of the national identifications. This would make it virtually impossible to remain in the US illegally, and anyone deported for terrorist or illegal entry reasons could not possibly re-enter the country through an airport or border crossing point with fraudulent documents. Visas would be issued by US Embassies in the normal way, with the addition of recording the applicant's biometric identity. Any person allowed into the country on a temporary visa would be immediately traceable if he/she stayed beyond the allowed period and made any financial transaction. Software to keep control of this should be implemented so that the process would automatically warn the FBI and local police when the visitor had overstayed.

Airport and border security checkpoints must be set up with advanced profiling facilities which would allow known, previously vetted persons of good character to be biometrically identified and allowed to pass through quickly. This would overcome the present nonsense experienced by people who unfortunately share the same name as a suspected terrorist, and are given the third degree every time they pass through security. It is also a crass stupidity that older people who have had joint replacements which set off the metal detectors should be given extra scrutiny both on themselves and their bags when passing through security checks. This diverts security operators attention from subjects who would more likely fit the profile of a terrorist to a person who would be the least likely to fit the profile. A much more secure checkpoint can be produced when the security equipment itself is able to decide how to test the person entering the checkpoint, and perform selected tests automatically. The technology to enable this is already feasible and should be implemented as soon as possible. I would recommend that an automatic security checkpoint is devised which tests the person simultaneously with tests to his/her baggage. One can envisage a checkpoint at which the first operation is to biometrically identify the passenger and check the identity against the passenger list of the day. If the passenger is known to be a non security risk, then only a minimum set of tests would be made on his/her person and bags. If however the passenger is unknown or known to be a possible security risk, then a bank of tests could be applied which may take a few tens of seconds to complete. These should include tests for weapons, explosives and nuclear materials on passengers and their bags. The use of electronic tickets will speed this process, since the system will have prior knowledge of passengers who are scheduled to fly on any given day, and will have time to check on the passenger's bona fides. The progress of the passenger through the checkpoint should be synchronized with the passage of his/her bags through the checkpoint, so that passengers and their bags are not allowed to proceed until all checks have been successfully completed. No passenger should need to take off shoes, since these can be adequately tested in a portal test, but coats and outer garments may need to be checked with the bags so that a more efficient check on the passenger can be completed. Advanced checkpoints would be integrated into a total security system which would integrate intelligence gathering with the checkpoint operations and response team control. Billions of dollars have been spent on software for battlefield control which advances our war making capabilities, but today, we are in far greater need of this type of defense in Homeland Security. After total integrated security is implemented at airports and border crossings, the system could be expanded to include other high threat installations such as government buildings, nuclear and chemical plant and national monuments. Unfortunately, casinos are much better equipped to pick out cheats than the federal Government is equipped to recognize and deter terrorists.

In past international conflicts, propaganda has played a part in influencing "hearts and minds". In today's struggle unfortunately, the Fundamentalists are making more ground against the voices of reason and tolerance. It has become conventional wisdom in the Arab countries of the Middle East that U.S. and Israeli security forces were the brains behind the attacks on the World Trade Center on 9/11. As ridiculous as this may seem to westerners, it is widely believed in the Moslem world that Mossad agents and Zionist sympathizers in Washington organized the attack to provide an excuse to invade Afghanistan and Iraq. Anything that non Islamic governments in the west may say or do to actively promote arguments against the worst aspects of Wahhbist doctrine only serves to make matters worse. The campaign to influence the hearts and minds of potential Fundamentalist terrorists should be made from within the countries concerned. The power and influence of the radical clerics must be countered by voices of reason. The voices of reason will however, be muzzled while radical mobs are burning homes of moderate Muslims or those of a different sect. We must somehow give them some hope of a better future. I have often been known to point out that nobody who had a mortgage ever became a suicide bomber. However, until the pendulum swings back, we must satisfy ourselves with passive defense and support any reasonable Muslims who may have some influence down the road. One of the key findings of the 9/11 Commission Report stated "Education that teaches tolerance, the dignity and value of each individual, and respect for different beliefs is a key element in any global strategy to eliminate Islamist Terrorism." The corollary to this is that we must be intolerant of any teaching which eschews violence.

We must also defend against the forces of radical Fundamentalism within Western cultures. It is an enormous inconsistency that Congress should disallow Arab investment in our ports, while welcoming the building of the Ibn Taymia Mosque in Los Angeles funded by King Fahd and staffed with Saudi Wahhabi Fundamentalists. It seems that it is not acceptable to compromise our physical security but it is acceptable to allow a foreign government to establish religious and scholastic centers which preach violence and hatred to susceptible young Americans. King Fahd and his Government have funded some 1500 Mosques, 202 colleges and almost 2000 schools for educating Muslim children in countries outside Saudi Arabia. The imam, Fahad al Thumairy, attached to the King Fahd Mosque in Los Angeles was an accredited diplomat of the Saudi Consulate until 2003 when he was barred from re-entry into the U.S. because of his terrorist connections. It was reported in the 9/11 Commission Report that "he may have played a role in helping the (9/11) hijackers establish themselves on their arrival in Los Angeles."

It is very likely that future Fundamentalist atrocities in America and European countries will be perpetrated by their own citizens. This has already happened in England, Spain, France and The Netherlands. It is the duty of every rational Muslim citizen to speak out against the venom and hate and fatwas which encourage violence against peace loving people. The convinced fundamentalists will probably not listen, but at least they should know that the population at large does not support their violent reactionary doctrines. Also everyone in the west should be aware that some Muslim charities are fronts and supporters of Wahhabi Fundamentalism. No one should donate to any organization that they do not know for sure are not supporters of extreme fundamentalist doctrines.

It took the best part of one whole century to contain and finally eliminate the communist menace. The success, when it came was due in large part to improved communications which convinced people in the Soviet Block and China that there was a better way. Muslim fundamentalism is a religious rather than economic movement but is still motivated by fear of change in the same way that the leaders of the communist block feared change. It may take a similar amount of time to remove the threat of the extreme Fundamentalists, but meanwhile we must improve our defenses against both their physical and ideological atrocities.

Chapter 10

Improving Quality of Life

Western Governments and civilizations generally have directed nearly all economic activity to improving Gross National Product (GNP). This has lead many people today to identify the pursuit of happiness with reaping as much for themselves as they can in their lifetime. There have been many studies to try and determine the major factors that make people happy, perhaps the most famous was made by Richard Easterlin of the University of Pennsylvania in 1974. Easterlin concluded that economic growth did not necessarily lead to increased satisfaction, and argued that relative income mattered more than absolute income. This has become known as the Easterlin Paradox. However, this has recently been rebutted by Betsey Stevenson and Justin Wolfers, also of the University of Pennsylvania, who have pointed out that since the Easterlin Study, far more data has been produced on the topic which seems to show that absolute income, on average matters more than relative income. In the quest for improved quality of life in the population as a whole, some Asian cultures based on Buddhist spiritual values emphasize more holistic and psychological factors. Gross National Happiness (GNH) is a term coined by Jigme Singye Wangchuck, the King of Bhutan in 1972 when developing a five year plan for the economic development of his country. The concept of GNH is based on the premise that true development of human society occurs when material and spiritual development occur side by side to complement and reinforce each other. The equating of high consumption levels with happiness by classical liberal economic theory is challenged by the proponents of GNH. I believe they certainly have a point, and the Buddhist practice of meditation has been shown to produce a happier state of mind. Researchers at the University of California San Francisco Medical

Center found that Buddhists who meditate regularly were less likely to be shocked, flustered, surprised or as angry as other people. I do believe there is a much more rewarding and honorable path to happiness than the selfish accrual of greater wealth. The feeling of well being experienced when we spend enjoyable times with friends or family for example, is much more valuable. This is a less selfish path to happiness that can be applied to the joy of belonging and contributing to a moralistic society in much the same way as an extended family.

In 2006, Adrian White, an analytic social psychologist at the University of Leicester in the UK, completed a world wide survey of 80,000 people to map out subjective wellbeing. He found that a feeling of wellbeing was most closely associated with level of health, prosperity and education. He found that in the happiness standings, Denmark came out top, which may surprise some since it is also one of the highest taxed countries in Europe. The high level of income tax reflects payments for healthcare, education, elderly and childcare services which are financed through taxes. At twenty third on the list, the level of satisfaction of U.S. citizens is quite good, but surprisingly, the Asian countries with large populations, China (82nd), Japan (90th) and India (125th) show considerable dissatisfaction with their lives. Not surprisingly, the countries wracked by internal conflict and political suppression come bottom of the list of 178 countries. Peace of mind is destroyed by the fear of financial, physical and psychological threat and the draining effects of chronic health problems. The frustrations of daily life such as dealing with traffic jams or filling in IRS tax returns feature less in deciding our level of well being, but nevertheless should not be ignored by government. In this final chapter, I will leave any proposals for the very important moral and spiritual development of society to the many faith based religions and to concerned citizens such as Eric Liu and Nick Hanauer whose book, "The True Patriot" points the way to a more inspired future. They claim that "It is time to rededicate ourselves to a true American patriotism, a civil religion of purpose that answers our deepest needs in this time of uncertainty." My own approach has been to try and devise new social structures and practices that will automatically discourage selfishness and division in society, and provide incentives to do the right thing. In this penultimate chapter, I will try to deal with the more material improvements which governments can make to improve standard of living and reduce threats and frustrations. I would like to point out however, that these would go hand in hand with inspirational and moralistic leadership that is recommended by others, some of whom I have recognized here.

The KISS (Keep It Simple, Stupid) principle can be applied to many aspects of our daily lives which would help reduce frustration and stress. Nowhere is this more evident than in the process of making one's tax return which, for many people is an annual dread. In chapter 5, I detailed a much simpler system which could be devised that would eliminate the need to make a tax return. It would only be necessary to total the net investment made during the year into ones Portfolio For Life (PFL) for the purpose of reclaiming the flat tax paid on that portion of income. Such a system would reduce frustration by reducing paper work and cost, at the same time as improving the fairness of taxation and the efficiency of collection of the tax due. This also leads to a better national identity and true patriotism.

Crime Prevention

Victims of crime and drug abuse are often reduced to severe depression and feelings of extreme vulnerability. Mitigation of crime can improve the well being of many potential victims and those under most threat from criminal activity. Arraigned against such criminal activity is a bewildering proliferation of police forces. I can see no advantage in having special police forces such as registry police, parks police or even University campus police. In Boston, until very recently when the Metropolitan Force was combined with the State Police, it was possible to come under the jurisdiction of one or more of Federal, State, Registry, Town, Metropolitan or campus Police depending on which line was crossed and what alleged offence had occurred. With so many police forces bearing responsibility for catching criminals and traffic offenders, it becomes nobody's responsibility to prevent crime. Cooperation, coordination and communication between various forces across the country are woefully inadequate. For example some of the radios of neighboring forces often cannot communicate with each other. My suggestion would be to streamline all forces into two, at State and Town (or city) level with efficient contact with each other and the FBI. Each force should nominate and train one or more members to be a liaison officer with other adjacent or superior forces. Mandatory exchange programs would also encourage better relationships and communication between different police forces. Improvements must be made in the ability to reduce crime by improving the way information is shared among forces, particularly in preventing terrorist acts and public massacres. The FBI itself must change from a largely crime solving organization to one which also prevents crime by gathering and disseminating information on a national and international basis. Better metrics for crime reporting are required so that both authorities and the public at large can see when improvements are made. Police officers themselves must become more computer literate, and more use must be made of the many software aids which can filter out irrelevant material; highlight important crime circumstances; collate evidence and search suspect files. DUI offenders for example must be kept off the roads by proactive policing once the offender has been found guilty. In another example, when a felon is found guilty of an offence which would deny him the right to own a gun, then the record should be automatically scanned to check on gun registration of the felon. If the record shows that the felon indeed has a gun registered to him, the local police could be notified and the guns confiscated from his possession. Similarly, when an application is made for a firearm certificate, it ought to be very easy to check the whole country for any offence which the applicant may have committed. This must also apply to people who have been found to be mentally unstable. Such was the case of the Virginia tech murderer who was allowed to purchase weapons despite being diagnosed as mentally unstable. In a future system of increased government responsibility, there would be no room for gun shows where guns could be purchased without any checks on the prospective purchaser. Providing peace of mind in the security of our work places and schools should not necessarily mean that we all have to pass through x-ray machines and metal detectors, but it will mean that our police forces will need to become more efficient and empowered to isolate the threat before it occurs. Individual rights should never come at the expense of the welfare and wellbeing of the community at large.

More time must be spent on prevention of crime, and less on other "fill in" duties such as guarding holes in the road. There is no reason why contractors working on roads and roadside equipment should not employ qualified, trained traffic control professionals to perform that duty. This would reduce the cost to the town and would allow the level of training and employment of police officers to be improved. During the nineties and early part of the 21st century, industry and agriculture has made remarkable increases in productivity, producing more goods with fewer employees. During this same period, police forces have increased their rolls but with some notable exceptions, have arguably become less efficient. Whenever there is an upsurge in crime, inevitably the call goes out for more cops on the street. It certainly has been shown that the presence of police tends to inhibit crime, but technology and better police practices can play a much greater part in policing which will help the various forces become more efficient at crime prevention. Bill Bratton, often referred to as America's top cop, described in his book, "Turnaround", how he achieved a dramatic reduction in serious crime, and halved the murder rate in New York City. He noted that "Crime, the theory went, was caused by societal problems that were impervious to police intervention. That was the unchallenged conventional wisdom espoused by academics, sociologists, and criminologists. I intended to prove them wrong. Crime, and as important, attitudes about crime, could be turned around. Using law enforcement expertise, leadership and management skills, and an inspired workforce, I intended to create an organization whose goal and mission was to control and prevent crime—not just respond to it." Bratton did indeed prove them wrong, and has gone on to do the same for the city of Los Angeles. There were many essential steps in the turnaround that was achieved, but one important aspect was Bratton's insistence of measuring crime statistics so that his forces could be efficiently aligned against the criminals, and so that it could be determined if the measures instituted were effective. The insistence on metrics caused several of the old guard to object that it was the job of police to be out on patrol, not sat behind a computer. Bratton retired the disbelievers and went on to impressive success. This project is one of the best examples of cybernetics in society. The metrics were made, the forces were moved to meet the threat and the loop was closed very successfully. Continuous improvement is also encouraged by honest data collection and analysis.

Technology can also play a more prominent role in police procedures. For example, the process of analyzing suspected drug samples at the moment may take weeks since the forensic departments are so backed up. By the time a positive drug analysis is made, the felon often cannot be found. Technology does now exist which can be deployed either at street level or police station that can be used by police officers themselves to perform an analysis in a few seconds and print out the result if necessary. By this means, the felon can be immediately charged and held in custody. The print out can be offered as evidence at the subsequent court hearing where it may not be necessary for the arresting officer to take the witness stand. If the defendant insisted on hearing the officer's testimony and subsequently was found guilty, he should be made to pay for the officer's time in court. Unfortunately, the purchase of such capital equipment at the local level is never easy since the competing demands on small capital budgets mean that this type of capital purchase never gets to be a top priority.

Another example of wasted time is when police officers are waiting in cruisers to catch speeding motorists. Traffic duty can be more cheaply and efficiently performed by digital cameras arranged in a system that automatically bills the offender. This would provide a net income to the town instead of incurring considerable cost. Unfortunately the introduction of cameras which are common in many European countries cuts out attorneys from the process. The argument that is preventing traffic camera installations in the US is that the use of cameras does not allow for legal "due process," and we all know that the lawyers must have their "dues". However, one can be excused for being cynical in a world where even the due process of Habeas Corpus has been compromised.

A culture of continuous improvement can be instigated in our police forces, and a reward system based on that improvement should be implemented. At the moment some police forces have quotas and bonus schemes based on the number of motorists fined for speeding offences. It would be better to install camera systems to mitigate speeding, and provide officer incentives based on reduction of crime and accidents. In this way, the Gaian principle of negative feedback would apply and more attention would be directed to improvement of our roads and to the safety of our streets, schools and workplaces.

The issuance of State driver's licenses has lead to abuses where drivers with multiple DUI offences have been able to obtain a license in another State. Illegal immigrants have also been able to obtain driver's licenses which in turn provide them with a legitimate identity. It would provide a much more secure system and an increased respect for the law, if driver's licenses were controlled by a central Federal License Office. This could consist of a central computer which could be accessed from the various State Registries. Each driver on file could be enrolled on a national data base secured by a biometric identity held in the central registry, but enrollment could be performed in a local State registry. The State registries would ideally be run by independent, responsible organizations such as Pinkertons that could compete to manage the clerical functions, organize driving tests, and provide biometric identification enrolment services. In this way, the frustrations of dealing with existing registry beaurocracy could be reduced. My own wife was cuffed and put in jail in New Hampshire for the simple reason that the Massachusetts registry had failed to update her record, which wrongly showed that she was driving without a valid license. On another occasion, I employed a service engineer to perform onsite services across the country. Unknown to my company, he had recent DUI driving convictions in two States, but had a current license in Massachusetts. I have personally been told of other poor service provided by some registry staff members that seem to have no incentive to provide efficient service, and certainly no program to continuously improve their service. The public would be better served by enabling this service to be competed thus providing less bureaucracy and more efficiency, accountability and responsibility.

Infrastructure

Some frustrations of our daily lives could be reduced by government investment in infrastructure which would also provide economic efficiencies. I will give a few examples to illustrate how more responsible government can act to improve efficiencies and reduce frustration and cost for everyone. For example the majority of traffic lights still have dumb controls which result in motorists burning gas while waiting at red lights when no traffic is passing through the junction. Many of these junctions would benefit from computer control, or being converted into mini rotaries. Such improvements in our infrastructure serve to provide employment and reduce long term expenditures for example on imported oil. Rotaries will not work however until unified traffic regulations are applied across the whole country, and motorists are taught to drive to minimum standards, and rigorously tested in driving skills and knowledge of the regulations. In contrast, the air lanes and pilot competence are governed by unified Federal regulations policed by the FAA. The safety of our skies is remarkably good, especially when compared with the death toll on our roads, so why has road safety regulation not been mandated at the Federal level? There is much room for improvement in the rate of injury and fatalities on our roads, which has provided great sadness and reduced the quality of life for many tens of thousands of families every year. According to D.O.T. statistics, over 42,000 people have been killed on US roads every year in the past 6 years. The death rate per 100,000 people has been steady at about 14.5 fatalities. This is twice the average rate of the major European nations, who have been steadily reducing the death rate over the same period. Some may argue that a reason for this is that Americans drive greater distances, but this is refuted by the statistics which show that less than half of the fatalities occur on highways where most of the miles are clocked. Lower driving skills and higher alcohol abuse by drivers may be a factor, but the safety of road surfaces, especially when wet, is nowhere near what it could be with the application of improved surface treatments that are in use in Europe. Unfortunately, Government seems to be unwilling to take on the responsibility of ensuring and improving the safety of our roads. It has been too easy to push the entire responsibility for safety onto the vehicle manufacturers who have done their bit in improving many safety features on their products. The quest for continuous vehicle improvement has lead to the development of air bags, automatic breaking systems, all wheel drive and other advanced safety features. In future, we can expect that in-vehicle radar will take some of the decisions away from the driver which could improve safety further, and might ultimately allow twice as many cars on the road as today. When can we expect Government to apply the same principles of continuous improvement to the roads themselves? I suggest that in future, one or more member of each US Embassy in the developed countries be tasked with reporting on their own experience and observations affecting road safety in the country in which they have temporary residence. These reports could be collated in the DOT, and possible improvements to US roads could be identified. Any action taken as a result of such surveys would both improve the safety of US roads and lead to greater efficiency in our infrastructure.

Many roads in New England are lined with trees on each side. Almost on a weekly basis, often on Friday evening, young drivers are killed after hitting a roadside tree or utility pole. Every time this happens, a police comment is inevitably made that it was believed that speed was a major factor in the accident. It never seems to occur to anyone that the utility pole or the large tree that was within a few inches of the road surface was the primary cause of the fatality. In the absence of a tree or pole, an accident may have occurred, but it would probably not have resulted in death. Many other accidents are caused by poor roadway and junction design. My own experience in Massachusetts has shown that at most intersections where there is a stop sign, the white stop line is drawn across the road at a point where cross traffic can not be seen for more than a few yards. Such sloppy attention to good road safety practice is inexcusable in our governing bodies. Even when one pulls out almost into the cross traffic, the lines of sight are frequently obstructed by walls, hedges, trees, and poles. I would strongly recommend that new federal regulations be made to define driver competence tests and minimum safety standards for road surfaces, verges, safety rails, sight lines at road junctions, road markings and road signs. Of course this would be easier to achieve if State jealousies were overcome by the abolition of State Law in favor of a unified federal system of law as was advocated in chapter 6. In Europe, with many different countries speaking different languages, they have instituted a standard system of icon type road signs which are immediately recognized in every country.

The maintenance of roads and bridges is another example of "if it's not broke don't fix it" attitude which has in the past lead to accidents and disasters. When government establishes a tax for a particular purpose, such as gasoline tax for road maintenance, then the proceeds that are collected should immediately be transferred into an account for that purpose that cannot be raided. It is a sound principle that those who use a service most should bear most of the cost, but gasoline tax is a much better way to finance road maintenance than tolls on the roads themselves. Road tolls are expensive to mount, interrupt traffic flow and require many local government employees. Gas tax also provides more incentive to reduce the consumption of gas.

As I write this, in the midst of one of the many winter storms which sweep across the upper mid west and north east States, thousands of people and households have been reported to have had no power for ten days. This is not the age of the pioneers who bore great hardship to open up the western part of the US. Today, people should be able to rely on the continuity of electricity supply that controls the temperature of our homes, provides light, powers our televisions and home computers, and keeps our food refrigerated. Losing power in mid winter can be disastrous if pipes freeze and subsequently burst. If we can afford to spend hundreds of billions of dollars attempting to prevent fellow countrymen killing each other in a country five thousand miles away, then we must be able to afford to give our own citizens the peace of mind and assurance of continuity of electricity supply. Here is an investment in infrastructure which will pay dividends in reduced maintenance cost and increased reliability. There is no doubt that all local power lines would be much more reliable if they were underground. Our neighborhood in a small town in Massachusetts has had underground electricity lines for the past twenty years. In that time, we have not had one power cut due to local disruption, but a large percentage of households in this and nearby towns have suffered multiple breakdowns during this period as ice and storms have downed power lines. We do not have to accept that we must live with this inconvenience, since all utilities can be run underground. Government ought to take the lead in setting standards for safe, underground installation of every utility service. It should not be left to each utility supplier to decide where to place the pipes or cables. Also, burying the services along roadsides should be facilitated by mandatory easement in roads or verges. If the Federal Government were to take the initiative and make investment capital available under very favorable terms to contractors to do this, they can insist on specifications for underground services in an efficient, combined service trenching and piping system. Different States may have differing standards depending on temperature or other local factors. For example, water pipes will need to be deep enough to prevent freezing. There is no reason why the utility supply system should not be organized in the same way as our roads, where the local town authority has responsibility. It is after all a natural monopoly since no two suppliers of gas, water or electricity install services in the same street. If a standard layout is devised and mandated, one contractor could install all services at the same time. One can even envisage a future system where all utilities are provided in one complex extruded plastic pipe arrangement with grooves and clips for laying in electrical and telecoms cables. If the utility companies did not actually own the supply lines and pipes, it would facilitate competition for all the services. The responsibility for the maintenance of the supply system could also be competed to ensure efficient response to any line failure. The capital cost of such a system would be similar to an aerial system, but the cost of ownership will be much lower than existing arrays of pipes and cables above and below ground which fail all too frequently. Dig Safe, the organization tasked with keeping all information regarding underground services would be an excellent organization to research and lead the initiative for such standardization of utility services. Not only would such a system of underground services be much more reliable, the resulting removal of all poles and unsightly wire-scapes from our streets will provide a safer, more pleasing environment. Coupled with this initiative, Government should encourage development of superconductive electricity service supplies by investment in research programs directed at producing superconducting alloys that operate at near ambient temperature. This may eventually allow suburban electricity services to be supplied at lower voltage and higher transmission efficiencies.

On this same tack, what can government do to alleviate the increasing cost of heating or air conditioning one's home? There is nothing more miserable than going home to a freezing house because the home owner cannot afford the cost of gas or heating oil. Unfortunately, the cost of crude oil is bound to continue to rise as demand from the developing nations increases and the cost of extraction in ever more inaccessible oil fields increases. Also the impact on the environment from carbon dioxide emission from burning fossil fuels must be mitigated. In chapter 8, I recommended the politically unpopular cause of building new nuclear power plant. Nuclear power is now competitive with oil powered electricity generation and has the added benefit of helping to balance trade by reducing oil imports. Government can help the development of more nuclear plant by removing some of the regulatory obstacles and passing legislation to facilitate removal of waste nuclear fuel from the plant. This is urgently required if we are to ward off the worst effects of global warming. Going a step further in this direction, I would recommend increased government investment in research to develop nuclear fusion reactors that could supply us with untold power for eons to come. This is not the blue sky project that it once was. Scientists working on the Joint European Torus (JET) have had some success in producing conditions in which hydrogen atoms fuse, releasing immense heat in the same way as the sun is powered. Dr Alan Sykes of the United Kingdom Atomic Energy Authority reported in a BBC interview in October 2001 "There are still very many difficulties but perhaps in a few decades we could have commercial fusion reactors in cities providing cheap pollution-free power." Investment in this type of project is much more likely to result in real benefit to society than some of the space projects that look for life on Mars for example. The way in which investment is made in such projects must however be improved by devising incentives such as performance bonuses or prizes for outstanding achievement. Government beaurocracies should never manage complex and sophisticated projects that rely on solving scientific and technological problems which may be open ended. Newt Gingrich in his book, "Real Change", proposed an interesting way of managing this type of project. He asserts that "the cost of being a major federal contractor is now so great and the contract timeline is so long that no entrepreneurial, market-orientated company can compete." The large government contractors have become almost as beaurocratic as the government agencies themselves. Unfortunately, this is in an area of industry which requires the highest entrepreneurial and innovative skills to ensure success and these are never found in bureaucratic organizations. Newt's solution is to offer substantial prizes for successful achievement. He gave an example of the NASA proposal for a manned mission to Mars that is estimated to cost $450 billion over 20 years. His solution would be to establish two prizes: a tax free $5billion prize for the first permanent lunar base and a tax free $20 billion prize for the first team to get to Mars and back. I applaud the principle in this proposal, but under the existing rules of accounting, no public company could carry the cost of such a project without showing a substantial yearly loss on the income statement. Nevertheless, I believe the proposal for stage prizes in a large research project is certainly worth investigating further.

Healthcare

I come now to what I consider the two most important features which government must change in order to improve the quality of life, not only for the many disadvantaged members of society, but for the future benefit of everyone. That is the provision of a higher standard of affordable education and healthcare. Dealing first with the issue of healthcare, I have not heard one voice in support of the status quo, but I have heard many Americans comment on how bad the national healthcare system in some foreign country may be, when they have no first hand experience of the country in question. It is my belief that the most important measure of any civilization is in the way that the society looks after the less fortunate members. We should all share the cost of providing healthcare, especially for those unfortunate people who are blighted by chronic illness or mental incapacity. This inevitably means that some form of National Health Service must be devised. There have been many proposals for improved healthcare systems in the US, every presidential candidate seems to have a different one. Most of the proposals seem to be driven by political expediency rather than to do the right thing to solve the problem. I do know that no proposal will be successful until the practice of defensive medicine is eliminated by removing the lawyers from the equation as was detailed in chapter 6. Also, when taxes are raised for a specific purpose such as healthcare, then those funds should immediately be transferred into another account which cannot be raided by the treasury for general Budget purposes. I am convinced that the essential features of any future health system will be the provision of choice and competition in all services. One way to achieve this would be for the Government to levy a tax for this purpose, and contract out health services in each State or groups of States to existing healthcare companies. Each company could be asked to bid on a basic service that could be defined in detail. Not all companies would bid the same price, but the lowest in any area could be chosen as the baseline and funded accordingly. The public could opt to go with another company which bid a higher price for the service, provided that they paid the difference directly to the company. This would operate in a similar way to the Medicare supplemental programs offered by many healthcare companies today. The cost of healthcare would likely be reduced by taking advantage of scale and competition and eliminating malpractice insurance. One can envisage an HMO type of system in which individuals could select the company they prefer to deliver the service from an allowed shortlist. They could also pay the healthcare company directly for improved services if desired. (e.g. reduced co-pay or making a change to a PPO system) The system should also incentivize people to be more accountable for their own health. For example, it is well known that obesity and cigarette smoking result in health problems. Unhealthy lifestyles should be discouraged and healthy practices encouraged by some form of incentive in the same way as careful drivers are incentivized by vehicle insurance companies.

Several countries in the world operate national health systems which are both cheaper and more effective than the healthcare systems operating in the US today. It would be of great benefit if a healthcare commission were set up to study several of the more successful national health schemes in Europe and Canada, to see what works best under differing conditions. It would be important for such a commission to canvas a cross section of the public in addition to Doctors, healthcare workers and government healthcare employees. The commission could then report back with its findings and recommendations for an improved healthcare system in the U.S. Not one of the national health schemes is perfect, but collectively, many developed countries have hundreds of years of experience successfully operating health services from which we can learn much. My prediction is that if this recommendation were to be implemented, healthcare costs in the U.S. would be halved, the level of healthcare will be improved and many who cannot afford healthcare today will be elated.

Education

Coming now to the subject of education, it will be to the benefit of everyone to have a well educated flexible work-force which can easily be redeployed from industries in decline to those in ascendancy. Individuals with higher education qualifications today can expect both higher incomes and more rewarding jobs. So with such strong incentives, why are our high schools failing to graduate only one third of students with the skills needed to succeed in college and work? Also, why is the drop out rate an alarming 30%? These are the questions that initiatives begun by the Bill and Melinda Gates Foundation hope to answer. Bill Gates, arguably the most successful entrepreneur of our age, and his wife have committed vast sums of money from their Foundation, and will in future dedicate much of their own time to addressing the world's greatest inequities in healthcare internationally and education in the States. At home, the focus of these initiatives is on improving the rate of high school graduation, particularly in the poorest districts that traditionally graduate fewer students. The project to improve graduation rates is a good example of a feedback control system in use socially. A change is made then the results of that change are measured to determine if the change was effective in making some improvement in the result which is sought, i.e. graduation rates. This will only produce significant national improvement however if the changes in policy and/or practices which have been shown to be successful, are then implemented across the country. The project will result in proposals for improvements which will be far more valuable than any proposals coming from theoretical educationalist study. All too often schemes for public school education have been implemented on grounds of educationalist dogma, most of which pay more attention to individual's rights than to good educational practices. I hope that some interim recommendations flowing from this work will be made quickly, particularly if legislation is required to change any policies. We also need Congress to recognize this project and take an interest in the results and recommendations, so that they can be reproduced across the country. Meanwhile, it is urgent that we give back to our teachers and school principals the responsibility to run their classrooms and remove the lawyers from the mix. Students cannot learn in an environment where the teacher is not in control of the class. Legislators should ensure that judges have the responsibility to safeguard our teachers' freedom to act in the interest of the class and of what is right. Judges must be impelled to make judgments that prevent frivolous law suits from going to court. Also courts should not be allowed to compel any teacher or head teacher to accept a disruptive or criminal student in their classroom. Any seriously disruptive student, or students caught bringing drugs or weapons into school should be punished immediately. Unfortunately, when corporal punishment was banned, no suitable alternative punishment system was devised. Corporal punishment worked to keep order in our schools for centuries, and certainly works to keep vandals in check in the pristine streets of Singapore. Either corporal punishment should be reinstated in our schools or some alternative to corporal punishment must be devised that answers serious behavior problems quickly and allows culprits a chance to complete their education. Suspension and expulsion only serve to push problems onto other overburdened services such as the police, probation and family services. Uneducated members of society inevitably burden the system with increased welfare payouts presently, but this would also be prevented by the abolition of all welfare as recommended in chapter 4. The imposition of no punishment means that the disruptive student can continue to disrupt the class and prevent the rest of the class from making real progress.

The problem of drugs in school must also be tackled seriously if we are to make any improvement in educational standards. We do not need to criminalize our youth, but we do need an increased determination to keep drugs out of school. Many school principals and school committees don't want to know how serious the problem is in their schools, since in many instances when drugs are found, both the reputation of the school and the career of some student is ruined. Inevitably, drug use and drug trade in school is far worse than any in a position of responsibility realize. Here again, a similar approach to that recommended for improved quality control can be implemented. In order to make any improvement, some way of routinely measuring the problem needs to be devised. For this, I would recommend that an annual or biannual sweep of every middle and high school is made to detect evidence of drug use. The result of the sweep could be published in an annual report card for each school. Recommendation for improvements can be made and the performance of the school staff should be measured on such improvements or lack thereof. My company developed trace drug detectors which could detect traces of illicit drugs at levels below one nanogram (one billionth of a gram) A billionth of a gram is the amount every person in North America, including Mexico and Canada would have if, for example, a one gram sachet of sweetener were divided equally between everybody. At this level, it is nearly impossible to use drugs and not leave a detectable trace. These detectors have been employed to wipe surfaces with a clean filter paper and subsequently detect residues picked up on the paper. The detectors are used for the routine detection of drugs in night clubs, schools and other institutions with great success. In one school, traces of marihuana were found on the catwalk above the theater stage, just below the extractor fans. This was a convenient place to smoke, since the culprits were hidden and the smell was not detected since the fan drew the air outside. In this same school, traces of cocaine were found in the music practice rooms. Other drug traces were found in one remote toilet and on one tree in the school yard. Recommendations were made; a lock was put on the ladder to the catwalk; the toilet area was provided with increased lighting; the school yard was patrolled and the music rooms were only used with supervision. On subsequent visits, No more drug abuse was detected in these areas. The essential points to note are that no police were involved, no culprits were targeted on the first sweep and drug use was reduced without resort to arrests or prosecution. Drug use was curtailed by the increased assurance that offenders would be detected. Of course, if the problem persists, the culprits can be detected by drug traces on their lockers and the police can be notified as a last resort.

Students who drop out could well experience boredom or frustration at their own inability to keep up. This could be countered by providing more interesting and relevant study topics. For example, if the proposal for a self run portfolio of investments were to be implemented as suggested in chapter 5, the best people to manage the portfolio would be the portfolio owners themselves. This would be facilitated by a very practical and exciting course of investment management in school. Schools would do well by setting homework to watch Jim Kramer's Mad Money evening program and to keep their own virtual portfolio for the years they are in high school. Prizes could be offered at the end of the school year for the most successful portfolio manager. I hope the research conducted during the Gates Foundation studies will include trying different curricula which would allow streaming between vocational and academic studies in high school. Many students are capable of learning in school what is presently being taught in college, particularly in the sciences where more graduates are required. Unfortunately, all too often the progress of the class is dictated by the speed of the slowest individuals. This policy increases the cost of educating students who would go onto college and/or university. Examinations conducted in high school at each year end should allow for students to be selected for steaming in the following year, with a possibility of accelerated acceptance into university. It has been my experience in life that the higher the goals that are set, the higher the achievements that are made. We must set higher standards in our schools, which in turn must be measured in examinations. The exam questions would best be set and the answers checked by some outside body such as a consortium of Universities which have a vested interest in the standard achieved. The children in school will surprise us by what they can achieve when we demand more. If we fail to do this, we will be on our way to becoming a second tier nation by the end of the century.

If the proposal to provide a Federal income for all adult citizens were to be accepted, one of the conditions for receiving the income could be achievement of a minimum level of competence in math and English. This would provide a powerful incentive to stay in school and stay out of any trouble that may affect the granting of their High School Diploma. Even the most problematic students will soon learn that the country can give them far more than they could ever steal from its citizens. Students who did not graduate could be given a second chance to earn a General

Educational Development (GED) diploma with further tuition in private school, community college or vocational school. Mentally impaired and special needs students could be awarded a graduation certificate with a qualification regarding their disability, but this should not prevent them from drawing Federal income when qualified by age.

The country has a vested interest to ensure that everyone is educated to the full extent of their capabilities, so that we can continue to compete favorably in the global marketplace. I strongly believe that we should all support our promising students all the way through university, by paying their tuition fees on selected, government approved courses. The voucher system would probably work best where a voucher for tuition could be issued to a value that amounted to the annual tuition at a reasonable cost university. The student would be free to choose his own course from a government approved list, at a university of his or her choice. If the course chosen was more expensive than the voucher value, then the student would need to pay the difference, or be offered a scholarship from some other source. Each approved course would be required to measure student's progress in yearly or semester exams. Any student who failed to make acceptable progress would automatically lose the government funding. Living expenses, books and other course material would be paid by the student. In this way, everyone who is capable of graduating from the course can be educated, and the country will be all the richer for this investment. The Treasury will no doubt subsequently recover the cost of each successful student's tuition bill in the flat tax which will be levied on their higher income expectations.

Chapter 11

The Way Forward

Several Western Nations, following the path of multicultural ideology, have proceeded to erode their own historical cultural background. We have become unsure of our own identity in a changing world where many new forces such as Islamic Fundamentalism, Gay Rights, Women's Liberation or the advocates of drug culture have thrust their own versions of the future onto a leaderless society. Historically, there have been several successful multicultural civilizations which thrived for many generations. The Greek, Roman, Ottoman and British empires for example, all had strong identities but above all, they had a tolerance for different cultures. The US people's acceptance of multicultural differences is one of the major reasons why people were able to work diligently together to make their country the most powerful and successful nation in the 20th century. I believe we can make advances and take democracy and civilization into the 21st century with new approaches and social systems without losing what was good and made the country great. We do however, need to refresh our national identity and stop apologizing for our own principles based on a strong work ethic and Christian values of forgiveness and tolerance. We should stop worrying about what is the politically correct expression to use and rely on our own values of respect for one another. Ronald Reagan, if he were alive today would be strongly advised against describing the old Soviet Block as the "Empire of Evil" as it would not be politically correct. However, everyone remembers the quote and the bold leadership it illustrated.

Today, the one thing we need to be intolerant of is intolerance itself. We should respect the rights of minorities, but we also need to guard the rights of the majority against the tyranny of vociferous minorities who want to change that which we hold dear. For example, if three quarters of the population want to continue beginning the day in school with a prayer, we must not allow a handful of people to stop it. We can however accommodate non Christians who would not wish to join the prayers. Our judges must return to the practice of making value judgments and do the right thing for society and not the individual who wants to win the lottery of litigation. Many people realize that the ship of State was headed in the wrong direction and it will take a gargantuan effort to turn it around. No single person can do this, but a movement can be started by a few concerned individuals that will result in a tidal wave of change. This process has already begun with new hope and enthusiasm following the election of the first colored president in America. In addition, a number of groups are beginning to make progress in starting a movement for change. The conservative group "American Solutions For Winning The Future" lead by Newt Gingrich is encouraging citizen activists to develop ideas for change based on the traditional Christian American values of accountability and good work ethic. Eric Liu and Nick Hanauer, who describe themselves as first generation Americans who are progressive and democrats are leading the True Patriotic Movement to a "higher call to country first". You are invited to join their website at truepat.org. The groups "Friends of an Article 5 Convention" and "Article5.Org" are working to get an Amendment Convention called so that some of the major issues requiring a Constitutional Amendment can be debated. Philip Howard is promoting the movement "Common Good" to "restore common sense to American Law". I would recommend all concerned and interested citizens to begin by visiting the websites of these organizations and join them if they believe in the goals of the organization.

Some of the proposals I have outlined here may require further research in University economics departments. Detailed analysis and metrics may be required to confirm many of my assertions so that more people will be convinced of the efficacy of the strategic changes proposed. I would encourage our economics and law professors to look at the proposals with an open mind and allow their most talented students to investigate some of the proposals in depth. Their investigations will be rewarded by a better understanding of society's problems and renewed determination to press for more efficient ways to address them.

My own thought is that many of the serious issues that we face today cannot be addressed by patching the system, but will require sweeping Constitutional changes to remove much of the inefficient and entrenched bureaucracy of government. Changes are also needed that will make for a fairer and more united nation of people of differing income levels and ethnic backgrounds. I do not believe that the existing status quo of privileged lawyers operating in the two party system can deliver the changes which will be required. If the administration of Barack Obama is successful in solving some of the daunting issues in his first term of office then perhaps the people will give him the two thirds majority in both houses of Congress that is necessary to institute the more difficult constitutional changes in his second term. He will need to steer his own Democratic party to embrace the best of Gaian conservative principles which tie rewards to work, and punishment to crime, but will also embrace the principles of a fair society in which the stronger shoulders bear the greater load. In the past, times of crisis in the US have produced exceptional leaders. Presidents Washington, Jefferson, Lincoln and Kennedy all rose to the occasion and saw the country through turbulent times. I believe that history will repeat itself and have every hope that Barack Obama will win his place among the greatest of U.S. presidents. To do this he will need to face the daunting issues with great determination, vision, integrity and energy to win the trust of enough voters to ensure a two thirds majority in the House and Senate. The people are ready for such a leader. The rest of the World is ready for the moral leadership of a revitalized America.